STEVE TILLEY

A YOUTH WORKER'S TALE

First published 2003

ISBN 1 85999 772 4

Scripture Union
207–209 Queensway, Bletchley, Milton Keynes, MK2 2EB, United Kingdom
Email: info@scriptureunion.org.uk
Website: www.scriptureunion.org.uk

Scripture Union Australia
Locked Bag 2, Central Coast Business Centre, NSW 2252, Australia
Website: www.su.org.au

Scripture Union USA
PO Box 987, Valley Forge, PA 19482, USA
www.scriptureunion.org

British Library Cataloguing-in-Publication Data
A catalogue record of this book is available from the British Library.

Cover design by Martin Lore
Printed and bound in Great Britain by Creative Print and Design (Wales) Ebbw Vale

For Geoff. You encouraged me to write.

Youth work resolutions

January

January 1

Why do I do these things? It's New Year's Day, 11.00 am. I'm crouched behind a dust sheet and surrounded by four mannequins. In a moment Kraftwerk's 'Showroom Dummies' will begin, Frank will remove the cover and my immobile colleagues and I will be revealed to the congregation. Congregation? This is the start of the sermon. I am about to be the preacher.

Over Christmas we have had a static display at the front of church - a crib made of plastic shop-window paraphernalia. It looked like a good idea a few weeks ago to surprise everyone on New Year's Day by taking the place of one of the dummies. Time to dust off the robotics and entertain the children. Then I can talk about the nativity bringing life and purpose to the New Year rather than remaining stuck in a tableau.

An hour later it is all over and the comments range from, 'Great sermon' to 'I didn't know you couldn't dance.' There's something about being a church youth worker that is a bit like being a gerbil. Nice to keep in the cage, fun to stroke but occasionally gives you a nasty nip. Have a bit of bleached hair and a couple of visible piercings and members of the church might invite others over to see the youth worker as they would invite them to see a new pet. I am as yet unpierced and don't care much for tattoos. I try to dress fashionably though. The rest of the church tends to be a hymn to acrylic.

St Mary's church building is so grand it manages to be anonymous, as indeed many churches do. It is over a hundred years old. Next to it is an octagonal church hall. It is surrounded by car showrooms, a supermarket, a civil engineer's office and a couple of units where they do unmentionable things with plastic. Once upon a time our church was a village church but Birmingham came out to meet it and carried on past.

The church building itself has rows of pews. There is a campaign to remove them and replace them with chairs but it hasn't really got up a head of steam yet. Given that the campaign to remove choir robes took ten years, removing something as fixed as a pew may take a century.

And the hall? There's a story. Twenty years ago a major fundraising campaign generated enough money for a two-storey hall: ground floor for youth work and first floor for posher meetings. Then some political shenanigans meant that so much money was used decorating the first floor and making it 'nice' that there wasn't enough left for a knockabout hall for young people. The ground floor (which is slightly below ground level) became cellarage and youth rooms. Young people are not allowed to play ball games in the nice hall upstairs.

January 2

Trudge is my name. I don't hate it or love it, I'm merely called it. I'm Trevor but only my Mum calls me that. My brother calls me Trev. At school my full name of Trevor Judge Gilbert was abbreviated to Trudge. I had one friend called Super Budgie the Atomic Amoeba and another called Drop-pigeon so it could have been worse. I wonder if theirs stuck too?

I first became interested in Christianity when I was invited to a church service some years ago. It was a Youth Service. At the time I remember being surprised that the people were mainly young, like me, and that the atmosphere was different. Different from what? Well as a child I was force-fed church. I spent most of the time on my knees, messing with what I now know to be hassocks. (These are not to be confused with cassocks, which are the long black dresses people wear when doing something important in some traditional church services. You would get into severe trouble for messing with them.) So as a child I thought church was boring. The Youth Service changed the way I felt. I went back to church the following week and, sure enough, it was boring. I have made it part of my life's work to stop Christianity being seen as boring. If my epitaph is 'Often wrong; never boring' then I'll be happy, although I just typed 'wrung' which sounds more interesting.

In the meantime I had met the curate from the church. Curate. Now there's an interesting word. Take it from me it is best not to worry about the history of it. Today it simply means Assistant Vicar. It is nothing to do with curator, although that is what many churches need. This particular curate visited me at home. He wore (whisper it) a leather jacket and ate a lot of my Mum's cake, poor chap. He argued with my Dad about the meaning of life and he watched tennis on the telly. I was impressed.

I worked in two churches before starting this job. There's not a great career structure for full-time youth workers in the Christian church but the job I do at the moment has no time limit. It means I can make five year plans and suchlike. But I am devastatingly broke. A mate is going to be thirty on Friday. These two sentences place me in a bit of a quandary. My commitment to take God seriously rules out major crime. My commitment to take friendship seriously should really involve gifts, meals out and him not having to pay for his own party.

All this because a few years ago I responded to a challenge to ministry and didn't fancy being a church leader. Certainly didn't want to wear a dog collar. But why youth ministry? Because I think presenting young people mature in Christ and preparing them for works of service is the most important job in the church.[1] I kept hearing about the church leaking teenagers – 300 a week in the 1980s. If the boat is sinking I want to be repairing the leak before getting more passengers on board. And with that razor sharp logic accompanying me I headed off to Bible College (my parents and some friends from my home church paid) to train.

I finally rose to a challenge issued to me by a girlfriend, that she wouldn't take me seriously unless I took God seriously. Sometimes I am grateful for the opportunity she gave me to think more carefully than most about the important spiritual questions that face us all. After all, if God was so important to her that she put him before me then I wanted to find out about him. Sometimes I think it's amazing what commitments people will make in exchange for regular sex. She still ditched me though.

My house is full of outsiders. I'm looking after John and Ruth's deaf dog. She is called Lass but she doesn't answer to it. She doesn't answer to anything. I've also got some of my friend Ron's furniture. He's going to America and didn't have anywhere to leave it. The biggest piece is called 'cupboard' but it doesn't answer to it.

The reaction to yesterday's all-age service has been surprisingly good. It is certainly the first time that the preacher has begun with two minutes of poor robotics. I was more pleased with the fact that the whole service was over within an hour.[2]

January 3

John says his dog has written a long list of complaints about the way she was treated and could I look after her again at Easter?

Spend three days planning and programming for the term to come. OK some of the time I do that. There are still some good movies on the telly.

January 6

Day off. Tell me this. If you wrote down a list of things your mother might say in response to the question, 'How would you like to spend your birthday?', how far down the list would, 'Go out and buy a new fridge,' appear? I don't think I'll ever understand women.

If you're going to have to spend the day buying a fridge you may as well throw yourself into the experience. I tried playing off two electrical retailers against each other with the cunning line, 'This FL56 is the same price at the other place so why should I buy it from you?' Unfortunately they didn't know why we should buy it from them, so we didn't.

Mum enjoys her birthday.

Having a party tonight for my mate Simon. I don't organise things to be deliberately evangelistic, but half hope that some interesting conversations might develop as our Christian friends encounter the unenlightened. To help this along we use three rooms in Simon's house, one for food, one for drink and one for sitting around in. What happens? The Christians all end up sitting around and occasionally send a runner for food. The others end up standing round the food and send occasional (no, make that regular) runners for booze. Very few conversations of theological value happen, although one guy, the husband of someone Simon works with, discovers that I work for a church and asks if I have ever met the Methodist Minister who christened him. The Christian community has some way to go before it is as small as he thinks it is.

January 8

Sunday again. I am the drummer in church. I'm surprised to find that I make a reasonable noise although the rest of the congregation sound like they have the hangover I have now recovered from. Susan, a vocalist in the group, feels very well until she starts to sing when nothing happens. Her lips move but no sound comes out.

Our all-age service (hooray for children's groups starting back next week) begins with the lie, 'It will only last an hour'.

Simon's party invitation said, 'Bring a dessert'. Today I go to friends for lunch and take six desserts with me. Excellent. There are 15 of us for lunch and I still bring one whole pudding back home again.

Our youth group starts up again in the evening and we have a good session with a few newcomers. We start a prayer-partners scheme. Everyone puts their name in a hat and draws out another name. Then they agree to pray for that person over the coming week.

We also get the members to make plans for the year to come and then to identify potential spiritual low points. We all commit to looking after each other on those particular occasions.

I'm having a bit of a spiritual crisis myself at the moment. Being responsible for Christian ministry is not a good place to be whilst having a spiritual crisis.

January 9

There is a Youth Committee meeting tonight. The committee is meant to support me in my work. It is chaired by Vernon, a very wise man. I have discovered that the more I speak at these meetings the more arguments I provoke, so I tend to do more listening than defending.

January 10

Do you believe that there is a loving God, who is involved in this world today? I only ask because from where I stand, there has been a shift in popular culture and most people don't believe that sort of stuff anymore. We haven't yet reached the point where people can clearly articulate why they don't believe, but most people don't. They do however believe in the forty million to one shot called the National Lottery. I have still not bought a ticket so when people ask if I've won, I say I'm £300 up (six years of not buying a ticket).

Rob (long-standing friend and difficulty-standing drinking partner) says the odds of winning the lottery through administrative error, that is without buying a ticket, are only marginally worse than if you enter. Well I'm convinced.

Meanwhile, God continues to annoy the champions of atheism, who think God is either a virus or an administrative error. The really tricky bit of God to ignore properly is Jesus. If you are having a spiritual crisis, check out Jesus. Read a Gospel. What happened to the body? 'Didn't you used to be dead?' is not something you can ask anybody.

That sounded evangelistic. Better get back to my own spiritual crisis.

January 12

Spend the day talking with other local full-time, church-based youth workers about the future of the church youth fellowship. There are ten of us. It is very helpful. A lot of people out there think the church is only interested in middle-class suburbia. It is certainly easier to run a fellowship model group with middle-class kids so we talk a lot about reaching young people who are more socially disadvantaged.[3]

The short walk back is not improved by my nose beginning to run and a slightly dry throat developing. I pray a prayer which goes something like, 'Lord, I know you're busy dealing with world poverty but could you convince me you are concerned for me by not making this cold last a fortnight like they usually do? Please. Pretty please.'

Get home, having shopped for food on the way. Watch TV and go to bed with Beecham's Powders. Day off tomorrow and I'm going to be ill. Triffic.

January 13

I think he does it to laugh at me. I wake up feeling doubly dreadful and then, within an hour of waking, feel better and better. Enjoy a lazy morning drinking coffee and reading magazines and then head for the city.

At the cathedral, they are making an old clergy friend of mine an honorary canon and, after a wander round the shops, I head for the service. I take a pen because I want to make a list of all the words that no one outside the church would understand. It is 'Choral evensong and the installation of honorary canons'. How's that for starters?

The cathedral grounds are probably the most valuable bit of grass in the city. In the summer, they are the host to thousands of office workers and their sandwiches, a few young lovers, several dossers and a couple of million pigeons.

To visit choral evensong is to enter the sheltered world of precentors and archdeacons.

After the procession of verger (caretaker), greater chapter (the other honorary canons), residentiary chapter (the canons with specific, cathedral-based tasks), provost (chief cathedral-based vicar), registrar (guy with a wig), churchwardens ('normal' people who look after buildings), bishop (big chief in the diocese (area of the country)) and bishop's chaplain (guy who holds his mitre (hat) crook (stick) and books (books)), I feel I have enough material for a small dictionary.

The provost welcomes us to 'this small but beautiful cathedral'. It looks like a galleried Methodist church with prettier pillars. The provost has the sort of stomach that clergy should have. It enters the church several minutes before the rest of him – a truly remarkable piece of architecture and construction.

Bill is duly and canonically installed without the aid of a safety net and his eyes don't even water. The provost insists on leading the new canons to their stalls (seats) by the hand, despite, I gather, their prior insistence that this would not be the case. Give a man a stomach like that and he starts to go power mad.

'They've made Bill a canon.'
'Does that mean we can get shot of him?'

January 14

Derby County, the other subject of my worship (I was born in Derby), get their first league point for several years by drawing with Forest. Further evidence that there is a God.

It's been a churchy week. In the evening I go to a buffet, bring-and-share, meal with the couples who have recently attended the church marriage renewal course. It is fun, although nobody brings and shares anything to drink.

January 15

I am preaching the first in a series on the Bible – 'What can we learn from the historical books?' I am embarrassed, as ever, by the positive reaction to my preaching. One woman is visibly disappointed that I am not preaching the whole series. I don't know what to do with this information. However, I am not so modest as to leave it out of this paragraph.

At the youth group, everyone is as high as a kite and unteachable. We abandon our plans and play games. Sometimes you have to do this.[4]

January 16

Single, male youth workers get invited out for a lot of meals in middle-class suburban parishes. Parishioners want to feed me up (and marry me off).

Tonight Richard and Jenny have invited me over before PCC (Parochial Church Council – the people in the church who make the decisions). Immediately after I arrive, I am given a comfy sofa and the family disappear in opposite directions to do homework, cooking and ballet classes.

Suppers out are much appreciated. I enjoy an interesting variety of hospitality. Often there are young children to be played with, animals to be petted and usually, because nobody believes single men can look after themselves, vast amounts of food to consume. Watch out for the Egon Gilbert guide to parish meals. This one is a superb prawn creole with home-made bread and (get this) a pudding. In my house, pudding is fruit, ice cream or yoghurt.

'Why don't you always come for dinner before PCC,' says Jenny. The thing about traditionalists, however much they hate to admit it, is that they are always trying to start new traditions.

The PCC is a lively gathering and highly motivated. OK, it's not. I write two poems and plan the next youth service.

January 17

Suddenly my list of things to do has slipped out of control. I never know how this happens. One moment I have plenty of space and the next I am stretched. It is probably a hybrid of poor management and laziness. At school and college, I was normally dismissed as someone who 'could do better'. Senseless comment. I have made a positive decision to do lots of things averagely. I can play several sports without making a fool of myself, enjoy varied reading habits, can play an instrument (OK drums) adequately, can cook, make people laugh, speak in public, run a small business (I've not tried this but I'm sure I could), decorate a house, help a house plant to survive – and these are only the things I thought of without trying too hard.

I suddenly remember, a little later, that I am a youth worker so I can referee several sports, beat the ratbags at table tennis and pool most of the time and clean gutters. None of these things explains why my list of things to do has gone critical. Or maybe they do.[5]

After a day which included two assemblies, a meeting with the vicar and some preparation for the weekend, I meet up with a couple of friends at the pub.

January 18

I am on the steering body of an organisation which arranges gap years for young Christians, so I have to go to London today.

The meeting is in that part of Victoria where people don't worry too much about leaving the Bentley on the road because they can always use the Porsche if it's stolen. Nosing into people's basements as I walk past their houses, I realise that this world is far from mine.

The meeting takes place in a church room next door to a choir practising for a memorial service. Some of the group say they may start crying because the music is so heavenly. I may start crying because it is so unearthly.

The rest of the meeting is interesting but uneventful and I manage to catch the early train home. I arrange my notes to do some Bible study work on Galatians. The lady next to me arranges her Bible notes to read the Psalms. This doesn't happen very often. Her name is Jean and she goes to church at an LEP in Princes Risborough. An LEP is a Local Ecumenical Project. It is a church run jointly by different denominations (branches of the Christian church). Jean's is Anglican (Church of England) and Methodist (Wesley's mob).

Old gag:

Will you come in for a glass of wine?
No, We're Methodists.
Well come in for a glass of meths then.

January 19

I run a residential camp for teenagers every summer. Tonight I am going to a church in the wilds of Staffordshire to advertise it to some young people and their parents. It is foggy and I miss all the landmarks from the excellent travel directions I have been given because I can't even see the side of the road from the car. Rob, my passenger and co-leader, says, 'I think that was a church,' so I stop. There is a knock on the car window and a voice says, 'Are you Trevor Gilbert?' This is another thing that doesn't happen very often.

January 20

My vicar has encouraged me to go to a preaching conference. It is a pity it starts on my day off but the train journey gives me a chance to prepare a five-minute exposition which I will have to preach to a small group.[6]

It's pretty nerve-racking stuff preaching a five-minute sermon to an audience of preachers. Thankfully my turn comes fairly early on and I don't have to spend the first night worrying about it. The sermon is not received too disastrously.

There is apparently a code at these events. When the leader of my small group says, 'You may well be right,' he means, 'I think you are wrong'. He tells me that Marks and Spencer sell trousers that fit, having spied my fashionably baggy jeans.

I discover I am sharing a room with someone I have never met before. This is always annoying at conferences, since most of us like our personal space. My room-mate turns out to be perfectly reasonable and pleasant. He neither snores nor farts. He washes himself properly and makes the tea on one of our two mornings. There is nothing wrong with him except that I wish he wasn't there and he wishes (probably) the same about me.

This conference centre has no bar. A brief chat with the bar staff at the local pub reveals the fascinating statistic that the record takings this year were once again provided by a national helpline's conference. It gave us a wonderful vision of a potential suicide being asked not to jump until someone had got the next round in.

January 21

The prospect of spending the whole day getting stuck into the Bible really appeals to me. I love doing it so find it hard to understand why I have to be reminded to.

I think I have discovered what the word 'hearty' means. We eat a hearty breakfast, sing a hearty hymn, respond with a hearty 'Amen' to two prayers and then listen to someone teach us. A bit more of the code comes out:

That's an interesting idea = it's rubbish
Can you summarise that in a sentence? = you waffled

It's an immensely windy day so a quick wander around outside involves taking more fresh air than I intended.

My room-mate is a kindred spirit and we talk into the early hours of the morning.

January 22

The preaching conference ends with a (you've guessed it) hearty lunch and I head home to report back. Discover that the church is still standing and there are some phone messages and seventeen emails. No one has sent me a huge cheque to thank me for my ministry.

Pop into the youth group to say hello. Later, I debrief with Rob over a couple of pints. Our code is:

Quick half = One pint
Half = Two pints
Pint = Two and a half pints
Couple of pints = Three pints
Few beers = More than three

This code has existed for a long time. Does everyone talk in code?

January 23

Although I had planned a quiet day to make up for losing my day off last week I am asked to come to the vicarage to talk finances. It transpires that getting a gap-year volunteer this autumn to help with youth and children's work is at risk through lack of money, even though it has been planned for ages. I manage to keep my cool (one of my specialties since I am too much of a whimp to show temper to a human, only furniture) and emerge with permission to go ahead providing I include some fund-raising in the preparation.[7]

January 28

By mid-morning my house is full of teenagers after a party at nearby friends last night. These guys are fun not work. OK they're work and fun. Are they my friends or my clients? Should I have another leader present when they come round? Probably, but sod it; sausage sandwiches for five.[8]

Two girls from the group turn up later and decide my house needs tidying. They move the stereo speakers somewhere more discreet so they can't become shelves again, ruining the sound quality. I'm almost tempted to go round to their houses and swap their hairdryers with the food mixer, but restrain myself.

Later I discover that my bathroom has been used by two of the lads to dye their hair red. Two towels ruined and probably some blame coming my way from their parents.

January 29

My sermon in the evening service is on 'sexual morality', a broad subject to tackle in twenty minutes but at least homosexuality is not on the agenda until next week. I begin with, 'Welcome to sex with Trevor Gilbert, and that's not an offer I make to anyone.' Not a titter.

My suggestion that God's first command to Adam and Eve was 'Get bonking' doesn't go down too well either. It overtakes a lead balloon as it plummets.

The youth group tell me they have been playing the *Countdown* hymn number game during the sermon. You try and make the final number on the hymn board from the numbers in the rest of them.

January 30

What better way to spend the coldest afternoon of the year than in Rob's garage sorting out the equipment for our summer venture holiday? Well that's a stupid question because if I were to write out a list of things to do on a cold afternoon then 'sort out the garage' would be about as far down as 'buy a fridge' would be down the 'things to do on my birthday' list.

Rob is a caver and he has introduced me to this sport. A worrying number of pairs of underpants (used) is discovered in the outdoor equipment store. Rob says they will be his. These pants are horrid. The deadly combination of mud and fear, I guess. And he's going to wash them and wear them. Cavers are nutters.

Questions for January

1 Colossians 1:28,29 and Ephesians 4:11-13. Do you find these helpful as the main aim of youth ministry? How would you state your aims, biblically, if not from these verses?

2 Is length the most important part of all-age worship?

3 Fellowship model youth ministry involves running a group with a core nucleus of Christians who invite their friends. Unless it has a really strong leadership and is very welcoming to outsiders it will struggle. Is this your experience? What other models might help?

4 Do you? Is there another way?

5 If you are a full-time youth worker, have you looked at the balance between time doing face-to-face youth work and time spent setting up, preparing, administration, tidying and explaining yourself to others at meetings? Does it get you down? What steps could you take to rectify things?

6 The whole 'time-off' thing can be a constant problem for those in ministry. How have you resolved it? As you follow the book through see if you think Trudge gets it right.

7 Do you find that youth ministry in your church is always being required to pay its way, even though it is ministry to those who can least afford it? How can the church be educated to invest in youth ministry?

8 Is it dangerous to be 'friends' with the young people in your youth group? Is there an obvious boundary between friends and clients?

Give up youth work for Lent?

February

February 1

Easter falls really early this year. The chocolate egg manufacturers had to start showing their adverts on Boxing Day. Next Wednesday there is going to be a big youth event at our church for the start of Lent. We are mixing Shrove Tuesday and Ash Wednesday to have, 'Pancakes and Penitence'. I need to finalise numbers from the other local churches, none of whom have replied in time to say they are coming. Several phone calls later I have managed to pin down only one of the other youth leaders. My professional colleagues are all brilliant with young people but hardly any of them nurture the admin skills to make their work effective. We have been jointly planning this event for six months now; how hard was it to remember to invite the kids?

February 2

My job description has no 'hours of work' section. I am paid to do a job instead of working a particular number of hours. There are several advantages to this. It enables me to work vocationally, single-mindedly and without one eye on the clock. I don't have to worry very much if borderline activities are work or not. There are two disadvantages:

Firstly, as a creative and diligent type, I am worth more on the open market than I get paid. Not being very good with money, budgets and the like I am usually very short of cash. My contemporaries, of whom I am not jealous, golly gosh no, all drive nicer cars than me and live in bigger houses.

Secondly it is only Thursday, with a busy weekend to come, and I have already done 42 hours of work this week.[1]

I have a coping strategy though. Some of the things I do which are work don't feel like work. If I play football with the young people's team (I'm an experienced, unfit midfield dynamo) or meet with other youth workers over a meal and a drink, it doesn't feel like work. But cleaning and maintaining the house feels like work. I try to make a distinction between demanding and relaxing work so that I don't go mad. There are bits of my job I'd do even if I wasn't paid. The fourth commandment is that in six days you shall do all your work – literally 'all that you have to do'. I need to make sure I don't spend my day off cleaning and shopping.

February 3

One of my bookshelves collapses under the pressure (I know how it feels) but the hardback copy of the *Canons of the Church of England* stops everything from falling down completely. A metaphor? And what was I doing in my office on my day off? Not saying.

February 4

I try not to do too much of my Sunday preparation on a Saturday but it has been squeezed this week. I am working with the 11 to 14s group tomorrow morning so need to have a chat with Jo, the main leader, to be sure I have understood her instructions.

Jo always questions things, constantly asking, 'What is the aim of this meeting?' Infuriating, but helpful, to someone like me who often draws the target after he has fired the arrow. If I don't make sure I've understood what she wants me to do she will be very disappointed. When she is disappointed she reminds me of my mother saying, 'Trevor, I hope you're doing something edifying.'

Once I have grasped the subject it is simply a matter of the best way to work chocolate and other treats into it, which is, of course, the secret of ministry to this age group.

February 5

Snow has a devastating effect on our church attendance today but a well-behaved 11 to 14s group is assured by the offer of time in the snow if they concentrate. We make a snow-vicar using a black bin liner and some foliage. You probably had to be there.

February 6

At our weekly staff meeting (vicar, curate, me and the administrator), we had a little space to sort out thinking and planning for the future.

We are trying to fix our plans for the next five years – 14 extra staff should do it. Empire building anyone?

As we leave, my vicar boss asks for a quiet word. He wants to know why, if I am complaining about the amount of work I have to do, I had time to change my computer screen saver in the parish office. He simply doesn't understand displacement activity as a key to creativity[2] and I want to have it out with him then and there. All I end up saying is, 'Is this about the snow man?' It isn't, apparently.

Lots of people are phoning about the Ash Wednesday youth event which leaves me with the need to improvise a solution to the problem presented by the size of our church building. Although it is a large structure with many meeting rooms it is only really designed for 150 in the church and, with a sound desk and welcome area, 125 is more comfortable. The hall will take 100 or so. I make a few calls and we decide to move the event to the Baptist church, which is far more versatile.

February 7

I never shop for youth events until the last minute. Some people think this is because I am disorganised. Fact is that this time last week I would have been buying enough eggs for 50 pancakes and now it is 250.[3]

February 8

The evening takes most of the day to put together. I instantly fall in love with Ray, the caretaker at the Baptist church, since his first words are, 'How do you like your coffee?' not the usual, 'I wouldn't park there if I were you.'

People arrive when expected and the event gets off to a lively start. We worship, led by a good music group, watch some video clips, take part in a guided meditation in groups with each group stopping for pancakes at different times and return together for a short talk on penitence. We read Psalm 51 and then Matthew 6:16–21 and take part in a symbolic act of making a mark on our bodies in ash as a sign of penitence. We encourage people to make the mark on their arms where it will not be seen by others, rather than ostentatiously on our foreheads. 'When you fast do not look sombre as the hypocrites do, for they disfigure their faces to show they are fasting.' (Matthew 6:16)

One of the volunteer youth leaders at the Pentecostal church is seriously distracting. She is called Becca.

By midnight, all the gear is unpacked. I sit down with a beer and make a few notes of what went well and what could be improved. Since I can rarely sleep immediately after a buzzing event, I watch the video of the night's football and fall into bed at 2.30 am.[4]

February 9

This afternoon, I help the diocese with an event for church leaders on youth work. It is a good session and several useful conversations take place over the breaks. Again and again I am struck by the amount of people who ask, 'What can we do about youth work?' My answer is, 'Have you got people in your church who are happy to take responsibility for youth work, or to be trained in it?' This is often seen as unsatisfactory, but frankly, if there is no one in your church who likes teenagers there is little point in trying to do youth work.

February 10

Junk food, reading and five-a-side football. Perfect day off. Then it goes into perfection plus when Becca and I bump into each other in Starbucks. She is attractive, single, female, Christian and a maths teacher. She hasn't seen the new Bond film and we agree to go together tomorrow night. A date. Well, that's a pleasant surprise.

February 11

Derby County win. The brief highlights on TV show a shot of the crowd after we score for the second time in the game. There is no applause or cheering, just shell-shocked faces trying to remember what to do.

The film is the usual rubbish. I find it difficult knowing how to react watching a sex scene whilst sitting next to someone I'd like to have sex with. Get on with saving the world Mr Bond please. Becca's hand is involved in a chance collision with mine on the armrest. Our hands end up holding each other.

As we walk to the car I comment on the chance meeting in Starbucks which Becca owns up to manufacturing. She had seen me go in so she decided to follow me.

'Do you ever kiss on a first date?' she asks. Before I have a chance to deliver any of the clever answers to this question I have been preparing for half my life, she pushes me against the wall of the car park, looks me in the eyes for a long time and doesn't kiss me. It is the most erotic moment of my life.

'What's your surname,' I ask her later.

'Bondd,' she says. 'With two Ds.'

February 12

One of our readers (person licensed by the bishop to preach and lead worship) preaches (talks) a terrific sermon (talk) on 'Understanding Paul' (the guy who wrote most of the last part of the Bible). It's the second best sermon I've ever heard from a man called Dick.

'Knowing You Jesus, Knowing You' is a chorus that was clearly written by someone unfamiliar with Alan Partridge and unaware that his middle eight was lifted from 'The Ugly Duckling'.

I have Sunday lunch with Jack and Evelyn, another of the church's backbone couples. They treat me very well and Jack turns out to be yet another person who owes his Christian commitment to Bash (real name Eric Nash). Bash started summer camps for public schoolboys in an attempt to train a next generation of Christian leaders. Jack quotes Bash, 'Damned Hitler's a nuisance; he's really interrupted the camp work'. Now that's single minded. In order to keep camps and houseparties for Christian teenage lads going during the war, Bash called them log-chopping or food-growing camps, since these activities were deemed essential during wartime. He could carry on with his Bible teaching in the evenings.

Sunday evening youth group is saved from ordinariness by a lad called Chris who describes discernment as, 'Helping with other people's Holy Spirit problems'. Brilliant.

February 13

Two assemblies, back to back. Paul, who is sharing the load with me, and I have a well-used assembly, which we put into practice today. I start in a dull way and then he interrupts, dressed as an outrageous quiz show host, ready to start asking questions about Jesus. He is supposed to interrupt within a minute, but today he holds up a sign at the back of the hall saying 'back in five minutes' and walks out. He's so dead.

In the evening, another week, another conference centre. A lovely venue with beautiful countryside, nice food and helpful staff, but it is one of the few places where I reach for the extra blankets out of the wardrobe. The radiator in my room refuses to respond to twiddling, fiddling or stern looks. Some more questions about conference centres. Why those bathroom tiles that look like chickens if they're a particular way round? Why those little shelves over wash basins that stop you getting your head right over the basin and mean you soak the floor when washing under your arms? Why those incredibly little basins that defy you to wash anything bigger than a finger?

February 14

This particular conference is for gap-year volunteers. I guess 100 or so volunteers must represent about the most committed young people in the country and it is great to be in their company. We discuss predestination and free will at the breakfast table, the problems of Northern Ireland at lunch and guidance over dinner.

During the afternoon, I am summoned to reception where a man is dressed up to the nines to deliver Valentine's Day flowers. He gives me a single rose. I tell him that if it is in his job description to sing he had better weigh up his preference between his contract and a punch in the face. Luckily he is only delivering. There is no note.

That evening I phone Miss Bondd.

'Did you?'

'Stuff did I, did you?'

'Well I, er…'

'They're beautiful…'

I didn't, so who did? And did she? And if not her, who?

February 15

Conference ends and I drive back. Tonight I have another Youth Committee meeting. This group of people are totally unlike me and so offer interesting thoughts and perspectives. I could regularly shoot the lot of them, but remind myself that the reason they are useful is that they see things in a different way to me. Vernon chairs it really well.

February 16

Woken at 6.30 am by a minicab stopping outside the house and a constant horn parping until I hear a door down the street slam and the sound of the taxi door shutting. Sleep is now gone so I get up.

The post includes a letter from a church newspaper wanting me to write a 'Diary of a youth worker' column for four weeks. £50 a week. A bit of common sense over spending it and that's a DVD player.

February 18

The young people from the church and I spend a happy day washing cars to raise funds.

February 19

Come as close as I've ever done to pulling out of a Sunday engagement at the last minute due to the arrival of the cold I thought I had shaken off. I wonder how helpful it was to spend yesterday permanently damp in the cold wind. I make it through using throat sweets and a big bottle of water within reach at all times. Don't do much justice to the youth group Sunday night meeting and, as ever in these circumstances, I wonder why I didn't take the day off sick. There are very few people who seem to get the 'sickie' balance right. The world divides into those who stoically come to work with their limbs hanging off or breathing life-threatening germs over everyone and those who take to their beds at the first sign of a dry throat.[5]

February 20

Not sure if today should be a day off in lieu of working Saturday, a day working at home or a day off sick. It ends up being a very unsatisfactory hybrid of all three, although I start to feel better. My nose is sore and dry but the sexy voice has calmed down, the throat is no longer dog-rough, I'm not tired or achey and Becca has phoned to see how I am.

Staff meeting isn't happening until Wednesday this week when we are going away for the day together.

Finances have escaped my control again (too much junk food) and there is a letter from the bank I really don't want to open.

I have discovered a lump on my back which needs to see a doctor. No illness for three months and then two things come along at once. Wonder if I can think of anything else to mention to the doctor when I see him. For a non-urgent appointment the waiting time is six days. By then I'll probably be fit again and the lump will have dropped off.

The doctor's receptionist asks which doctor I normally see. Good question. When I tell her I don't normally see doctors she fails to find it amusing. I confess to being registered with Dr Jolly (great name). He is indeed the doctor I don't normally see.

February 21

Derby County win away. Nothing else matters.

February 22

Twice a year, the staff team spend 36 hours away from the church to talk, think and pray together. It is a time for sharing ideas and planning, with a 'team-building' element to it. Whereas large company teams go paint-balling or dune-buggying, we share bread and wine and ask God to help us in our work.

Due to circumstances beyond anyone's control (the vicar has to attend a very important conference) we are only having one day together rather than stopping a night away. Today has been referred to for the last few weeks as our '36-hour day'. No one finds this the slightest bit strange.

My cold (day four) is causing nasty pressure on my sinuses and the lump on my back is starting to hurt. Time to reread Job I reckon (Bible book concerning a guy inflicted with sores, amongst other things, to test his faith).

February 23

My house bears the scars of the youth group on half-term. The kitchen is a disaster, every room has a different noise source, the air is filled with essence of feet and there is no food in the house. I love them.[6]

Ben, 16 years old, probably wants to be a performance artist of some sort. His latest scheme is to drive around the district with a TV and photograph it in different places. This will demonstrate how we all watch TV but never look at the design of the case, only the programme on the screen. He can't drive yet, so guess who has to risk arrest to carry this out. OK I don't have to; I want to.

Cold, day five. Call me Mr Snotty.

February 24

As it's half-term, I get to spend most of the day with Becca. We take our overdrafts to a few Cotswold towns for some stretching exercises.

February 25

Iggy Pop is on the telly. He performs in a pair of see-through trousers and no underwear. He later takes the trousers most of the way off as the picture fades. By the squeals from the soundtrack, which isn't faded, he does go all the way. I used to have trouble getting my Dad to understand popular culture. With this, I wouldn't know where to start. And if I ever accidentally let the PCC see this programme I think they would probably call the police.

February 26

Holy Communion, sometimes known as The Eucharist, is, at best, a delightful way to remember the body and blood of Jesus Christ. At worst it is a meaningless ceremony full of excess where everyone becomes more concerned with getting it right than remembering what it's for. The Church of England is not the only church that suffers from ecclesiastical inertia;

that is, it continues to do things long after everyone has forgotten why they do them. That is why I found the simple sharing at last Wednesday's 36-hour day so much more helpful than any Sunday morning service.

One of the youth leaders arrives with a moustache because, 'I didn't have time to shave everything'. We all delight in telling him that it's only the bits that show which need to be shaved.

February 27

It's finally the day for the doctors. Like the rattle that remains stoically silent before the mechanic, my back is lumpless and healing. Since the lump has recurred in the past, I go ahead with the appointment and meet Dr Jolly. I have an endomorphic cyst (I can say it but I'm not sure I can spell it) which has to go. Having survived wisdom teeth extractions and a scalpel in the unmentionables a few years back, I reckon that there are few things they can do to me under local anaesthetic that would deter me from turning up. The appointment is for two months' time.

Cold, day nine. Only one handkerchief today and some sensation in the top lip.

My mobile rings during staff meeting prayers, which is one of the things my vicar hates more than anything else in all the world. I swear he'd invite Satan round for supper as long as he turned his phone off.

Questions for February

1 How do you feel about work? Do you have an old-fashioned 'trade union' approach to it, that you do your hours and your job description and no more, or are you a servant of the church and available to help with anything? If there is a balance between these extremes, where does it lie?

2 How can you best support creative people in their ministries? What are the ideal conditions in which you can be creative?

3 Should we be more ruthless with asking people to book for events, or continue to absorb the stress that flexibility requires?

4 What time of day do you work best and how can you, if at all, work your life round to using that time well?

5 Does it? If so which camp do you fit in?

6 What rules do you think you should set up if you use your house for youth ministry?

Not Spring Harvest...

March

March 1

The cold has gone, after two weeks, hooray! Why is the whole church sneezing? You can't take two weeks off work with a cold can you? Everyone else is looking in my direction and suggesting that if I had, they wouldn't have been ill. If I take two weeks off I get back to two weeks work and there is no way round this.

The Breakfast TV female presenter is wearing a skirt instead of trousers today. This makes it officially a good day.

Out at the pub in evening (three times now) with Dave and Trish. Dave argues that marriage is only proper if there is a public commitment in a service or similar; I say that I don't know any other way to treat my brother and his partner than as married, since they have lived together, without getting married, for fifteen years. Realise, with some hilarity, that as Dave is not a Christian and I am, it would be usual to be on opposite sides in this argument but we are on the wrong opposite sides. We both agree that the problem is not marriage but weddings, which needn't be costly, overseas or white. We also agree that 'boyfriend' is a stupid description of the man going out with Dave's mother.

March 2

Harry, one of the young people from church, comes to see me because he has had the cost of a newspaper docked from his first ever wage packet as a paper boy. The newsagent said he failed to deliver a Daily Mail. Harry disagrees, saying the paper was not in his bag, but the legal rights of a paper boy are minimal and the newsagent won't budge. Harry has to go along with it or resign. Life's lessons come thick and fast when you're 14. I decide not to intervene, as it will only make his life worse for the next few weeks, even if I do manage to get him the money back.

Later, I attend a training day for summer camp leaders. This includes a gruesome piece of training by the St John's Ambulance Brigade in which my small group encounter a girl with a compound fracture of the lower leg, which has bone sticking through the skin. How do people manage to go straight from this to their lunch?'

March 4

Today I am in awesome administrative mode. This happens occasionally. I unexpectedly get enthusiastic for filing, desk clearing, chasing up and generally getting things done. You have to go with the flow on these days so I change my priorities round a bit and end the day with a wonderfully clear desk, arranged diary and planned work.

March 5

Mothering Sunday. The church group for 11 to 14s was called LAZER. They have recently voted for a new name and have decided to call themselves Brian. They are taking the morning service. It is a little livelier than usual although one or two of the choruses are a bit twee. I'm getting too old for songs with actions. No that's wrong. You're never too old to make a fool of yourself. I simply don't like them. We give a bunch of flowers to every woman in the church, mother or not. We have a Mothering Sunday and then go out of our way to avoid offending non-mothers.

Drive over to offer gifts and presence to my own mum. I have specified a light lunch, which turns out to be ham, chicken, pork pie, salad, garlic bread, ordinary bread, wine, beer, fruit, cheeses and coffee followed by chocolates. Dad then falls asleep in front of the rugby game he has been looking forward to all week. At half-time, my brother and his partner arrive and cheer up the afternoon. Mum spends the whole time we are there interrupting, changing the subject, walking off in mid-sentence and complaining that I never tell her anything. She even butts in when I am answering one of my dad's rare questions to say that I never tell her any of my news. I think it is amazing how normal I have turned out, considering. Many of my family are the sort of people who end sentences with the word 'considering'.

Normal? Ha, that's rich.

Becca and I spend the late afternoon walking and talking until it gets dark.

Still haven't told my folks about her.

March 6

To make life choices at 13 is tough, but tonight is Options evening at school, where several members of Brian have to decide which GCSE subjects they will be studying. These days you can do short courses in film making and rock music plus GCSE photography if you want. Eeeh lad, when I were that age it were all work and no 'rock music' courses. What is school coming to? (It's getting better actually). One or two of them pop round first for a chat as they haven't been able to persuade a parent to come with them. The first time one of them came round to talk about something like this I asked, 'Have you spoken to your parents?' I discovered that Dad was long gone and Mum had two younger children to cope with and a series of 'clients' in the evenings. Our area is a huge social mix and some of the parenting is pretty inadequate.[2]

I use my usual technique of asking a thousand questions to get the young people to think. I try not to answer any of theirs. I am in no position to advise them on their choices but I can help them weigh up alternatives.

The youth team meet for supper. We manage some work too. We use a bean bag, a plastic dog, a pint of milk and a clock to help us think creatively about teamwork. Then we read Luke 10:1–20 together and look at the way Jesus sent his workers out. We notice they get a big vision for the work, 'The harvest is plentiful, but the workers are few' whereas we often undersell our work when we are looking for volunteers in order not to scare them. Hmmm. 'I offered to help out with the children on a temporary basis twenty years ago and I'm starting to wonder what temporary means,' my imaginary friend says.

March 7

I have offered to be in some drama for a children's holiday club at Easter. At the rehearsal, I discover that I have to play the lead (Captain Kirk) and there are four pages of script to learn for each of four days. The exploding job description gets me again. More deadly than a landmine.

The rehearsal is a bit of a disaster. We have no director so nobody takes charge. I hate this. My friends tell me I always fill any leadership vacuum. I don't like leading things, but I like it less if nobody is in charge so I tend to take charge. I love being part of arrangements that are well led by someone else. Anyway, with no one attaching movement to words it is almost impossible to learn the script, and there are three more scripts to learn.

March 8

Receive a nice email from someone who has read my first column in the national church press. It is so encouraging that someone read what I wrote and enjoyed it that I resolve to drop a line to any writers I enjoy in future.

March 9

Take the drums to the local primary school. Fantastic day getting to know the children and encouraging them.[3] Some are naturally rhythmic. I guess families around the parish are soon going to be hating me for introducing drum practice to their lives.

March 10

Day off. Watch three movies and go out to a party with Becca and some others in the evening. I walk back to her house. Over the last few weeks we've done the first kiss and the first snog with tongues. I sound 13 not 30. Now every fibre of my being wants more.

March 11

Prayer day for the leaders of our summer camp, We (13 of us) spend four or five hours eating, studying the Bible and praying together. It is a fantastic privilege to be able to ask the creator and sustainer of the universe to help you on your holidays. God made our campsite, a boarding school, so he's the best person to ask how to use the place effectively for his work.

March 12

I play drums, help with Brian then go to lunch at the vicarage. Then I lead the evening service, go to the youth group (but don't have any specific responsibilities tonight) and have cheese on toast for tea. This sounds like one of those 'What I did at the weekend' children's stories, doesn't it?

After the evening service at church I learn that there are eight, not four, Captain Kirk pieces.

March 13

At the staff meeting, it becomes obvious that Becca and I are now public knowledge. At 30 years old (we are the same age to within a month), they will be marrying us off. I ask for my colleagues to hold back. They say they will. They look like they won't.

March 14

I regularly attend two meetings in London. I go to one of them today and for a change I take a bus across London. The advantages (nicer view than you get from the tube) are balanced by the behaviour of some young people on the top deck of the bus with a sachet of barbecue sauce (don't ask).

This meeting is the board of directors of the organisation which runs my summer camp. I am on the board as a trustee. I find it hard to believe that I managed to become director of a limited company before my 30th birthday. Fellow directors include a barrister, several high-powered management executives and a senior clergyman. This doesn't mean to say that the position has any financial rewards attached to it apart from travelling expenses.

I would describe my faith as 'hanging on by my fingertips' at the moment. It was heading for rock bottom, but has, I think, flattened out. I'm banging on the seabed a bit, but don't believe I can go much lower. Was that more than one metaphor? It sounds a bit introverted but I spent a lot of the train journey struggling with it.

On the drive home from the station I am uplifted by hearing a football result which begins, 'Derby County 4' but the 'up' is only momentary since it is followed by '... Watford 4'. What a team.

Update on lottery tickets. I have now bought three. Wanted to know what it felt like. I don't only want to cure my own problems but would like to buy a permanent campsite and a Derby County midfield player.

Update on football result. Derby County have bought a foreign midfield player who scored on his debut and made some of the other goals. Winning lottery money to be diverted to defence.

March 15

School RE lesson on suffering. I introduce the subject with a short talk: 'Christianity is the only religion I understand to have anything to say about suffering. The focal point of the Christian faith is the death of Jesus Christ on a cross. The cross was a barbarous weapon of death, used by the Romans to make an example of any who opposed them. Shortly after Jesus' death, even a Roman centurion is quoted as describing Jesus as the 'Son of God'.

'This completely pointless suffering of the innocent one shouts much louder than the suicide bombers who die for Allah or the many faiths that call us back to look deep inside ourselves. It won't be comforting to the parents of innocent children, shot in their school gymnasium during an ordinary Scottish school day, or those whose office work was interrupted by a plane coming through the window, or those whose church service was disturbed by a maniac with a sword, but it is clear the Christian God identifies with the sufferer more than the perpetrator.

'I am fortunate. I moan about money, relationships and the way decisions my parents took sent me down a road I wouldn't have chosen myself if given all the facts. I have suffered the bereavement only of my grandparents and two or three dogs. Bereaved parents whose children have been abused, tortured and murdered will spend a lot of the rest of their lives asking, 'Why?' They won't get an answer. This world is a mess and, in the absence of a cross, largely purposeless. What amazes me is how come the world is not more violent, more depressing and more cynical than it is. I can't fathom reasons for goodness without Godness too.'

I meant to start a discussion but create a profound silence which takes some effort to turn to something interactive.

Towards the end of the day I discover that I have inadvertently offended a church member with something I wrote in our parish magazine. It was my attempt to be humorous, in a bit of a rush. I apologise, because I have no wish to fall out and it was a badly crafted paragraph that caused the offence, but I still struggle with why people take offence so easily. I don't think I do. If you know that the person who offended you doesn't normally do so (we have worshipped together and got on well so far without falling out), then surely the assumption must be that they boobed rather than went out of their way to annoy you. Ah well.

March 16

Laws governing church leadership and ministry:

1 **Law of strategic indifference** By choosing to do nothing exciting in a particular area of ministry – for instance always being boring at 8.00 am Holy Communion – it is guaranteed not to be a growth area. This is not to be confused with:

1a **Law of convenient myopia** Deliberately choosing not to pick a battle which would be both time-consuming and controversial, even though it is a matter about which you fundamentally disagree.

2 **Law of piggy-back whingeing** Whilst members of church councils or leadership teams are getting at you about something they will take the opportunity to get at you about something else.

3 **Law of cyclical proficiency** Churches gain experience and ability in one area of ministry but lose competence in others, previously learned.

4 **Law of disjointed incrementalism** Best expressed as an example: 'We gave £1,000 to them last year so let's give them £1,100 this year.' This law is not necessarily entirely bad. It saves everything having to be discussed again every time. Sometimes (ie with the national economy) the matter is so complex that radical change is too risky.

5 **Law of phantom consensus** 'Vicar, people are saying...'

6 **Law of title inflation** 'Curate' becomes 'Director of Evangelism' (telling other people about Jesus).

7 **Law of occupational obscurantism** 'Caretaker becomes 'Verger' and 'Window Cleaner' becomes 'Transparent Wall Maintenance Engineer'. Applied to places, 'The Dump' becomes 'Household Waste Reception Centre'. Applied to inanimate objects, 'seats' become 'pews' and 'tissues' used at communion become 'paper purificators'.

7a When applied to theological concepts this becomes the **Law of intentional obscurantism**, but that is the subject of another article.

8 **Law of non-proportional continuity** In the church, it is far easier to start something than to stop it.

9 **All-age service, fixed-ending falsehood** Inflate all announce-

ments concerning all-age service length by 10–50%.

I appear to have used the morning as an opportunity to write down all my current thinking in this area. It was, up until this morning, all contained on the back of a small paper bag from a Country Craft centre.

Today is a preparation day, which is why I was so displaced and did the previous piece of work. I am spending the whole of Saturday on training the youth team and some guest leaders from other local churches. I have left today completely blank in my diary. Now even on a completely blank day, I reckon two hours work will come my way through the post or via email or the telephone. For that reason I need to crack on with the prep. (And it also means that on any given day, if I plan seven hours of activity I am going to end up working for nine hours plus.)[4]

March 18

It's a bright and early start for a Saturday in order to get the church lounge set up by 9.30 am. I meet up with my old colleagues, with whom I worked a few years ago, Pete and his wife Margi. They are going to help.

At the training day, I don't recognise a guy who has put on a few pounds since I last met him. I manage to keep the conversation going for long enough to remember him. Why don't people introduce themselves and assume they have been forgotten? It's far more polite.

March 19

Palm Sunday. Pantomime donkey. I'll say no more.

March 20

I have managed to end up with the responsibility of rewriting all the scripts for our holiday club drama. Nobody else could do it so I was lumbered. At least it was something to ponder during the staff meeting.

When I come to do it it isn't so bad. By the afternoon, I finish that and another job I had not been looking forward to. I achieve this by rewarding myself with a biscuit and a computer game every time I finish a sketch. Rob refers to these jobs as 'eating slugs'. They taste disgusting all at once, but in small enough pieces you can manage them.

March 21

And so onto the coach for the church outing to Spring Harvest. I've not thought about it at all and am not entirely sure I want to go in my spiritual state.

It is a dirty coach. Arrive wanting a shower. Find our chalet. Change mind.

March 22

I have no responsibilities here except 'to be refreshed' according to my vicar. I try hard but all the banner waving, and arms-in-the-airing and slight hints of over-sincerity leave me colder than I want to be. I gravitate towards the youth tent and play pool with a couple of 17-year-olds who are there so against their will it is untrue. Why do Christian parents do this? I go for a coffee with the lads (who are really, honestly, called Ben and Jerry) and discover they are clergy kids. We get on well and they agree to come with me to the late-night entertainment. I'd like to say that they then repented on their knees before the Lord, but we exchanged email addresses and I offered Jerry a bed for the night when he visits Birmingham University in the autumn for a look round. Considering his slightly crusty, skateboard dude look I try not to look too surprised that he intends to study classics.

March 23

In the 'most repeats of a single chorus' competition a strong front runner is today's new song. We learn it before the meeting. We sing it two and a half times during the meeting and at the end we sing the whole thing through twice, then have an instrumental verse and chorus, then repeat the chorus three times (second time without backing music). Wonder if that's how Wesley taught 'And Can It Be'? Maybe there's only so many times your chains can fall off in one song.

March 24

Good Friday. Surprised to find that I miss being in my home church.

March 25

Have stayed up too late most nights but, notwithstanding previous comments, return feeling vaguely refreshed for having been out of the parish for a few days. The letters' page of the church newspaper for which I have been writing is divided equally between those who think I am a waste of space and clearly not a Christian and those who say it is the first piece they turn to now. It is strange to read such aggressively anti letters given that my column was meant to be a light and momentary distraction from depressing church news.

March 26

Easter Day. It also coincides with British Summer Time adding to the sleep deprivation problem. I sleep through the sunrise service but manage to get to church for the morning service and praise God through my personal fog, content with the absence of ministry responsibility myself. Worship for the non-hypocritical:

Leader: The Lord is risen
Response: You may well be right

When your Christian faith is at a low ebb it does not pay to think too deeply about the origins of the universe. Consider the resurrection of Jesus. That is the place to start. If Jesus is the image of God then he is the place to look for clues, which means looking, carefully, into the Bible and studying it, talking about it, reading books about it if you are able. If this life is not all there is then the best clues are in the resurrection of Jesus Christ but, as Paul says, if you conclude that he is not risen then everything else the Bible has to say becomes irrelevant. What is the point of goodness in this life if it is all there is? I hang on to the promise that death is not the end.

I wish the preaching of the resurrection at Easter was better. Because all our major festivals these days are celebrated with all-age services we don't seem to get much more than kiddies' talks. Meat please (but not bull).

My mum and dad come round for Easter. Dad smokes the house out and Mum talks gibberish. She confesses that she has considered doing a Mensa test. Managed not to laugh in her presence.

I was a member of Mensa for a year. Complete waste of time and money but the kudos was excellent. Mensa members are not supposed to brag about it. What's the point of that then? I need to brag to survive.

In the afternoon, John and Ruth bring Lass round. She heads straight for the place where I put her food bowl last time she was here. Nothing wrong with her memory then. By the end of the day, I am asleep in front of the television. I wake up in the early hours of the morning covered in dog.

March 27

Bank holiday, Ms Bondd, dog, country walk, perfect.

March 28

Frizz! is a unisex hairdressers on the High St. Ems cuts my hair. We get on well. I'm not very good at establishing relationships in a hair salon, especially a unisex one, but frequent attendance makes it a more comfortable place to be and I've got to know the staff.

I think that all sorts of institutions, like schools, hospitals and yes, especially churches, feel strange until you get to know the routine. All church leaders should be required to go to places with which they are unfamiliar every now and again – how about all starting in a bookies?[5]

Ems has split up with her boyfriend and he has moved out. Daniel (the manager and stylist to the rich and ugly) has earnest conversations with all his clients, holding forth on a variety of matters and occasionally conducting a conversation in which the whole shop can partake, as long as we understand that he has the last word and is always right, however bigoted his views. I tell him he should have a pulpit fitted in the salon.

Jools is a senior stylist and the most sensible of all, apart from the thickness of her make-up. She is a little overweight. Make-up must account for a lot of the bulk. She was recently married and the parish priest tried to rip her off with excessive wedding fees. I think I might have helped the reputation of the Church of England by being the one that squealed on him (I told Jools what the fees should have been as I have them in the front of my diary) and he has been removed from that parish by his bishop (so Jools tells me). Then there is Roy who is so camp he should work in a Guides uniform. He'd probably think that was a good idea. He dresses very dramatically, in Max Wall type leggings and lots of clingy, yellow tops.

I could go and queue at the local barbershop (number two back and sides, scissors on top) and save two thirds of the bill. I could, but I don't.[6]

March 29

Young people's outing to the cinema. I enjoy the film while they text each other. Afterwards we empty into a local café-bar for smoothies and lattés.

March 30

In the evening, I wander along to a meeting at the local junior school. Along the road from my house there is an area of public open space and the council are suggesting renovating an old playground and turning it into a skateboard park. Brilliant idea. It will keep all the local skateboarding community, some of whom I am getting to know, from terrorising the public in the car park and on the shopping centre steps.

However it becomes clear that local residents think this will make the area unsafe. One woman says, 'I was nearly attacked the other day and I felt so scared because it was dark and empty. Imagine if the place was full of young thugs.'

In the absence of any skaters turning up for the meeting (bit much to expect given the reception they would get), I stand up and say, 'Most skateboarders are ordinary, harmless kids, not young thugs. Wouldn't you have felt safer with a load of young people around and some bright illumination like the council are planning?' Apparently she wouldn't and everyone in the neighbourhood agrees with her. I anticipate bricks through my front window any moment.

I head back to church depressed and with several hours of painting scenery still to do for the holiday club. Ben is there, alone. He has been all day. He is so committed it hurts.

March 31

Wake up in the early hours of my day off to a knock at the door. It is my next door neighbour, a dear old woman, recently widowed. She is shaking. Someone has thrown a brick through her window. It has 'no skaters here' written on it.

Questions for March

1 What practical training have your youth team had? First aid? Food hygiene certificates?

2 Trudge has a lot of young people 'pop round' to see him. Should this be encouraged?

3 What talents or skills do people in your church possess that could be used to build relationships with schools?

4 How well do you manage your work? How easy do you find it to say no?

5 Where could you go to get the idea of how weird it is to walk into a strange, new place?

6 Do you feel in any sense critical of Trudge's spending priorities? What would you say to him?

Holiday club

April

April 1

Despite it being a morning when there is no need to get up, I am, unusually, wide awake by 7.00 am. I think the phone rang at 6.45 am, but I may have been dreaming. I eat a leisurely breakfast and watch a video of the week's football. Nobody has managed to fool me by midday.

Preparations for holiday club (starts on Monday) are going well and the church hall has been turned into a fire risk with bin-liners and spray paint to make it look like the inside of a space craft.[1]

April 2

At church, Ben asks why I didn't answer the phone yesterday morning. He had gone to a lot of trouble to fake an accident where he had fallen off his bike on his paper round. He'd done fake blood and everything, but as I didn't answer the phone after five minutes he gave up and went home. 'You weren't stopping the night at Becca's were you?' he asks. Five minutes. I must have been tired.

April 3

'Welcome to St Mary's holiday club. Everybody say, "Yeah!"'
'Yeah!'
'There's nobody there, we may as well go home. I said, "Yeah!"'
(*Roof-raising volume.*) 'Yeah!'
'Oh you are there.'

Thank God for pantos.

We have rehearsed our space soap opera so much we have ceased to find it funny, but the kids do. It goes well, as do the music and the games.

April 4

The format of our holiday club has been particularly effective – an hour-long, magazine-type presentation first thing and then workshops on art, craft, football, games and drama. Each successive day, the kids have arrived more excited to hear the next part of the soap opera, the next verse of the rap and have identified with two main characters, both dressed as space travellers. It is fun to watch everyone trying to fit into the space theme. Some manage, others don't exactly carry it off. Working in front of children is a matter of confidence. If you want to be a children's entertainer you've not got to care what you look like. One or two people make the mistake of asking rhetorical questions and are then faced with a load of kids with their hands up trying to answer them.

I am well impressed with some of the older teenagers, who throw themselves into the club and make excellent helpers, small-group leaders and generally contribute to the smooth running of the whole thing.

April 5

After a straight-forward, incident-free holiday club I go home to watch a video as I have no responsibilities from lunchtime onwards. Planned to re-watch Reservoir Dogs. Ben is at a loose end and asks if he can join me.

I decide that to all intents and purposes Ben behaves in an adult way so, rather than him watching an illegal copy in some dodgy friend's bedroom, I let him watch it with me. It is an excellent film; more like a play than a movie since it is mainly set in one place with flashbacks.[2]

Very relaxing afternoon, including reading the whole of Q on the day I bought it.

April 6

Lass is happy and the lawn is once again beginning to be a dog toilet. Still, the flea-ridden cat who normally basks on my patio got a surprise when I opened the back door this morning. I will now have the joy of a cat-free garden for a few days although Lass trashed my few daffodils in scaring the cat off.

I still have the cupboard that Ron left me. It is in my cellar and behaving well. Ron's letters from America suggest I will be keeping the cupboard for some time.

Holiday club includes a medical emergency (girl with asthma attack) but we have thought first aid through well. While someone phones her home for the inhaler she has forgotten, we lie her over a bench and get her breathing into a paper bag. Learnt that on the first aid course. Well chuffed. By the time the inhaler arrives she is feeling better.

April 7

Last day (oh no it isn't – oh yes it is) and we send everyone away with an invite to bring their parents etc to church on Sunday for a special celebration of holiday clubness with free gifts and food.

April 8

Derby win away at Leicester and my least favourite Leicester player is taken off with rib injuries after ten seconds. Wish I'd been there.

April 9

Lass has been no trouble at all. She leaves today. She is so deaf every time I come down in the morning I scare the crap out of her (technical term).

Church is absolutely packed out and many parents turn up who wouldn't otherwise be around. There are presentations of certificates to the children and thanks to all the people who have worked so hard. I have really enjoyed it because I have not been in charge but have been able to be up front and to do some writing for it. Although my part has been no bigger than that played by many other people I am given a small gift and thanked in person, publicly. I feel compelled to share the gift (chocolate) with the other members of the drama team and am embarrassed at being singled out in such a way. I secretly enjoy it too. Two faced? Yes, both of me.

Lass goes and I hoover the house and beat the rugs to a pumping drum 'n' bass soundtrack.

April 10

Motivation to get down and do some work is very low – always a problem for me after big events. It's coming-down-from-the-mountain time. Today I meet a volunteer who might be coming here to do a gap year for the twelve months from September. I don't seem to know what I'm supposed to be saying, looking for or promising, so my technique of total bluff is required. No problem. I find her (for she is a she) very articulate, a Christian and anxious to learn about youth work. Also gorgeous but I mustn't let this affect my professional judgement. I tell her she is welcome to come to St Mary's and scrape my tongue off the floor.

I wish I had more time to spend on cinema, live sport, videos and books. I am committed to having very little spare cash for as long as the church wants me to do this job. I'm not completely broke but have to be careful. A windfall would do very nicely, but I've given up lottery tickets. I found that using the same numbers every time led to a compulsion to buy a ticket, in case this was the week. My numbers are 4, 11, 29, 30, 44 and 45. Four birthdays and two consecutive numbers outside the birthday range. Now I've stopped buying tickets I must remember not to notice the winning numbers – I can't imagine how I'd feel if my numbers won a fortune and I wasn't in the draw. Good reason to use random numbers I reckon.

A drink with Rob is called for tonight, which he tells me I will have to subsidise. I've steered clear of him for a few days because I knew he was embarking on a difficult piece of work in his garden that required the assistance of friends. I am his best friend, but there are limits.

My vicar has gone to Africa for a fortnight. Vicars do things like this.

April 11

We've started a Bible study for older teenagers for this term. It's designed to help and encourage them through exam season and to allow them not to have to come to anything else we do. Only three people tonight, but what a fantastic discussion we had. I introduce John's Gospel by showing the verses where John gives his own reason for writing 'that you may believe without seeing' (John 20:29–31).

April 12

Had a scale and polish at the dentists. Always a joy and so nice to part with cash for it too. My dentist has a new toy, a small camera, so she showed me the back of my teeth on a TV screen. It was bad, man, it was bad.

Worked out my financial position and discovered that I had put down one credit item twice and one I thought I had received I hadn't so, as ever, I'm more broke than I thought I was. I never discover accounting mistakes which work in my favour.

If I could sort out my tax position it would get better, but I can't afford to pay my tax consultant.

I keep bringing home a particularly rare sort of basil plant from the supermarket. It is designed to die the second it enters the kitchen although looking fairly healthy in a shop display cabinet.

April 13

Every now and again, I go for a long wander around the neighbourhood as part of my work. You notice things when you wander instead of walking purposefully or driving. I pray for people working in the anonymous offices on the retail park. I try and guess which of the council houses are now in private ownership – one clue is that people always change their front doors as soon as they can. I keep one eye out for young people who should be back at school by now.

April 14

Completely out of the blue a letter drops though my door. It is from the parents of a member of our youth group – Melinda, a delightful girl. They complain that I have put other young people on rotas for reading in church and singing in the music group and ask why their daughter is being overlooked. 'Is it because of the colour of her skin?' they ask.

This is hilarious, or would be if it wasn't so serious. She has such light skin that only now, reading the letter, does it occur to me that she may be mixed race. I have never met her parents; they don't come to church or any of the parents' events I put on from time to time.

The comical thing is that if she has any Afro-Caribbean blood in her then it excludes the genetic material that supplies rhythm and pitch. She is also a hesitant and poor reader.[3]

Whilst I am already drafting the reply in my head I have learned, from bitter experience that it is best to take time over these things. I also need to take advice and, in the absence of a vicar, phone the Diocesan Youth Adviser. The DYO can see me in the morning or not for a fortnight.

As I have to think work this morning, my mind wanders to the deadline for the youth budget. Help, gosh, crikey and disaster. It was due last Wednesday. I check back in my diary and see it clearly written in.

I go on to work straight away on the budget and by mid-afternoon I think I've cracked it. Today was a bad day. Not the sort of bad day that Bruce Willis has in *Die Hard* movies, but bad enough. Becca had a bad day as well so we were great company for each other by mid-evening.

April 15

The Diocesan Youth Officer, who is always helpful but not on my theological wavelength, listens to my story. He asks if there are other young people the same age as Melinda who are also not on any rotas. There are. He thinks I will be OK but suggests that once the speculation of racism has reared its head it is very hard to recover a balanced position. He says the Diocesan Chancellor provides legal advice and he will get an opinion and get back to me. I want to go and see the family but he advises against it telling me instead to drop them a note thanking them for their letter and promising a reply in a few days.

During yesterday's bad day, I broke my watch on the gear stick. A small bit of plastic has chipped off which means that the strap will no longer attach to the watch itself. The watch is a complete unit so the case cannot be replaced but I can have a voucher against a new one if I wait for two weeks. No watch for two weeks. There's a challenge.

I have a wedding to go to this afternoon. These days weddings seem to take for ever, and that's not only the case for those couples who've lived together for years before deciding to go all official. Even Christian weddings seem to take forever. Rick and Kate married at 3.00 pm and the speeches finished at 9.25. I know because I kept looking at my missing watch and then at the clock on the wall. I drove home as they were thinking about starting the dancing. I survived endless photos, 45 minutes of speeches (the groom's was funny though) and a long, badly-served, vegetarian meal with small portions and no seconds.

Today is National Constipation Day. I thought you ought to know.

April 16

After the events of the last couple of days, which have really shaken me, it is a joy to get back to some youth work again. Brian are particularly responsive and get my feet back on the ground.

At the youth group, Melinda sidles up to me and apologises for her parents. All I can say is, 'Thank you.' I try not to stare but notice that she has a faintly olive complexion.

April 17

Staff meeting is cancelled due to lack of business. I mention reviewing Easter and the last few weeks but the curate doesn't think this is worth a meeting. He's leaving soon but I think he's already moved out mentally. I spend today working at home, meaning I can have my perfect working day. I plough through until a late lunch and then have a long break before working again at the end of the afternoon.

April 18

After time in the parish office dealing with messages and papers, I settle into some reading for a few hours. Maybe it is because of some of the parishioners, maybe the residue of a protestant work ethic but I feel guilty if I spend time reading. How can something I enjoy so much be work?

Our Bible study group carries on working excitedly through John's Gospel, this time starting right at the beginning and looking at the Word made flesh. We are taken aback by the idea that no one has ever seen God but Jesus shows us what God is like.

April 22

A free Saturday. Fantastic. One of the disadvantages of having a job that operates on a six-days-a-week basis is rarely having a weekend, or even two consecutive days off. I enjoy taking Friday as a day off because I hardly ever have to get up early on Saturday mornings. My aim for Saturdays is not to go looking for work but if there are appointments, events etc then I do them. I try to get any preparation done in the week.[4]

April 23

'It says on the rota sheet that a member of staff is leading the prayers today.'
'Yes, that's right.'
'So who is?'
'Whichever member of staff was asked.'
'So who is it?'
'I don't know.'
'Who does?'
'If anybody does, I do.'
"So nobody has been asked?'
'No.'
'So it's you or me?'
'Yes.'
'And you're preaching?'
'Yes.'
'And I'm a member of staff?'
'Yes.'
'It's five minutes until the start of the service. Shall I do it?'
'Is my hair looking O.K?'

I thought I'd write this down word for word. This is the sort of stuff that happens in ministry. I improvise the prayers.

April 24

Today, I need to do most of the week's work because I'm on a training course for two days. I need to prepare for a training day on Saturday and catch up with the business that three days away has left. I am very grateful to people who have offered to cover the Bible study tonight at the last minute. Why have I left it until the last minute to ask anyone despite having been booked on this course for nearly six months. The longer I left it the harder it got and the more apologetic I had to be to ask. I hate myself sometimes. I also hate the telephone. I notice, not for the first time, that I am happy to ask virtually anyone to do anything to their face but hate ringing them to ask. Why?

The vicar is back. He is full of Africa.

April 25

Excellent first day of a two day course on presentation skills, run by an ex-army management consultant. The materials and technique are impressive – bit down on sensitivity and listening skills, but one of the best trainers I have had for ages. The few of us from the diocese who bothered to attend (and yes this is a bit arrogant) were probably the best youth workers in the diocese. The ones who are hopeless didn't bother. That's why they are hopeless I guess.[5]

In the evening, the holiday club team head out for a pizza together. Went despite the fact that I couldn't afford to and a lovely lady called Maureen (recently widowed, very well off) picked up the tab for all twenty of us. I feel the occasional hint that God has got my money in control. Someone recently borrowed my car and left petrol money to cover precisely the amount I needed for shopping on the way home. I wish it was always that straightforward.

April 26

Day two of the presentation skills training and a chance to prepare a presentation, present it and video it. It is great fun and very helpful at eliminating errors, bad habits and helping with the bit of preparation where you organise your material. It doesn't save you research time, but getting the researched material into shape will now be much easier. It will help me to 'push the filling to the edge of the sandwich'.

The trainer tells me I will find things a lot easier if I buy a cheap watch. It's because I owned a cheap watch that I'm having to do without one.

St Mary's annual church meeting is uneventful. Spy a guy my age who I don't know, sitting at the back. I invite him for a drink afterwards. He turns out to be a potential new curate, who is visiting to see what we are like. During my second pint I start to tell him the truth. Then I become conscious he may not want to come so I start spinning it a bit. He's OK.

April 27

The youth workers' five-a-side team, for whom I made an excellent debut last season, have a practice tonight. This is a new departure for the team, who normally need introducing to each other before every match. There is a competition for local youth groups next month and the full-timers feel it is their duty to enter and win. (The young people feel it is their duty to either show us up or injure us.)

By the time I arrive at Becca's house I am so red-faced that she thinks I am blushing.

April 28

Despite considerable amounts of warm-up exercises yesterday, I am pretty stiff. Deciding which bit of my body to move first is like a golfer making a club selection. The knee? No, the ankle. Maybe the foot.

Spend the rest of my day off having the cyst removed from my back and then sitting in a chair as the anaesthetic wears off. Try to cure the pain with some single malt.

April 29

And so to the first opportunity to use my new-found presentation skills, at our children's team training day. My job description is for working with 11- to 19-year-olds but it stretches in both directions to cover children and students. I have been asked to help the team think about their vision for the work. It goes well, even though I say so myself.

In the evening, a monster Chinese takeaway for 14 is excellent. I haven't laughed so much for ages. It hurts the stitches.

April 30

Music group in church has only two musicians and I am one of them. Still, Jane the saxophonist/clarinettist makes up for it and I play a lighter percussion that usual. It looks as if all our sermons from the vicar for the next few years will start with, 'When I was in Africa...'

Questions for April

1 How safe, really, is your youth/children's work?

2 Do you go along with Trudge's logic here? The movie has an 18 certificate and Ben isn't.

3 Consciously or unconsciously, are you bothered by the demands of political correctness? As a concept, is it useful at all?

4 Does this seem OK to you? Or should church employees take two days off? Trudge has already mentioned that he is paid to do a job not work a certain number of hours. Based on your reading so far do you think he works too hard/not hard enough/about right?

5 How much time do you devote to training? How useful is it? How do you achieve a time balance?

Everyone's doing exams

May

May 1

May Bank Holiday. I'm a bit thick about nature and stuff. So when I ask Becca what that white stuff is that grows in hedgerows about this time of year I am genuinely surprised to learn that it is may, or blackthorn. Is that why May is called May, after the may flowers? Clever or what?

Today is a free day for Becca and me so we visit a National Trust House. I'm getting so old that I agree to become a member. We take out joint membership. Why? We don't discuss it; we just do it.

First barbecue of the year. Rob once put out a barbecue with paraffin so I am always surprised when they go well. This one went well but it was too cold to eat out for too long. The counter staff in the off-licence only work one evening a week each. They all seem to recognise me though. Funny that.

May 2

It is my annual review at work. Two hours talking about myself. Gorgeous.

The potential curate comes for a meeting with the vicar after a staff lunch. He is the second candidate. The first (came last year some time) was one of the most tediously boring people I have come across for ages. She had a diverse and interesting CV and yet appeared not to have managed to learn to have anything to say about all the experiences. Pity the church that gets her.

Next up is called Pete. In front of the vicar, he asks me if I have sobered up yet. Then he winks at me. I hate being winked at but it is a wink exchanged between two people who are going to get on. Always judge on first impressions.

Get a new watch. Hooray.

May 3

A men's magazine prints an edited-down version of a letter I wrote complaining that they had characterised Christians as dull and out-of-touch. I wonder if I'll get any stick for it from some of the more uncuddly Christians of my acquaintance. The word 'screwing' is not one you hear from many parishioners unless they are doing DIY and I put it in the letter. Mind you it's not the sort of magazine most of them read. Not top shelf but probably should be, or would have been a few years ago. I win a book token.[1]

Evening sees another football practice. That's us ready to do battle then. Not even stiff after this one.

May 7

All-age service preaching boosted by presentation skills training, with all the visuals targeted at the 5% I want people to remember. I also use the senses of taste and touch (well movement anyway), to help hammer home the main points. I repent of using visual aids that emphasise things I'm not saying

Vicar adds a largely irrelevant crossword puzzle which takes ten minutes and emphasises things we aren't saying. It also means we take ten minutes to learn a short Bible verse. Sometimes we make the simple things in life complicated. Is that why no one learns much at church?[2]

May 8

It is my birthday – I am going to see a boy band with 5,000 screaming girls. At least Becca is coming too. At the last minute, I learn that the two girls in the youth group I am taking (which is why I agreed in the first place) have offered lifts to two people. Six in our car is a bit of a squash and probably illegal. Becca sits in the boot bit of the estate and lies down when police cars are near.[3]

Great curry for two afterwards. We set a timescale for meeting each other's families.

May 10

It hasn't happened to me before but today my flies break and I have to go home for a change of trousers. Luckily, someone cancelled an appointment due to illness or there would have been no space in the day and the safety pins would have been a right pain every time I needed the loo.

The phones have gone off in the church office and the computers keep crashing following little local power failures. There is a bloke opposite the church, with a mini-JCB, who at least has the decency to look embarrassed.

Turns out that the youth room trip switch was the cause of the problem, not the bloke with the excavator (so why was he looking coy?). One of the light fittings is full of water but we don't know why. People look at me as if I ought to know. Perhaps I should.

May 11

Terrible news. Our first football game is cancelled because the others cannot raise a team.

May 12

Harry's friend Raj's fourteenth birthday ('I'm for 'een now'). I'm invited to a party in the evening because parents will be away. I get over the thrill of being invited to a 'parents out' party after all these years and come to my senses in time. I could end up being blamed for a lot of bad things. It is also my day off. Politely decline. Pop round with a card before it starts.

Loads of the kids in the youth group pop round these days, which is good, although I encourage them to come in twos unless it is an emergency. I tell them regularly that Friday is my day off, but they never remember. One or two retain the information but decide they are not work: 'I know it's your day off Trudge, but we only came for a chat.'[4]

May 13

Boring, boring cup final. Back in January, Derby departed in round three to a third division team. Rob's son, Jason, aged three, got frustrated that we were watching football, not him, especially when we asked him to be quiet.

He threw building blocks on the carpet (quietly), stomped out of the room (quietly) and slammed the door (quietly). When we asked if he was all right he said, 'I very noyyed with you!' Our laughing didn't help.

Becca and Rob's wife, Trudy, sit in the kitchen talking about nothing except people and drinking tea. Women do this kind of thing.

May 14

Confirmation. This is a service (which a bishop attends) in which those baptised as infants make their promises for themselves. They 'confirm' their baptism promises. Two of the candidates have not been baptised so we quietly baptise them before the service and then make confirmation the central focus. This is ridiculous.[4]

Ben is confirmed in a Black Rebel Motorcycle Club T-shirt. 'Apart from the trainers it's my most expensive article of clothing; it cost £35 at the gig.'

Mark is confirmed in shorts. He is a hardy northerner who comes to church thus clad from April to October, exposing his substantial thighs.

Vicar has done the confirmation classes, not because he doesn't trust me as I have done a couple while he was away, but because he likes to get to know the young people. Good for him.

There are some strange bits of Anglicanism. If you don't pay attention, you can hear a bishop say 'tortoise' not 'taught us', 'Peter God' not '... be to God' and 'our souls' sounds altogether wrong.

Guess what? We sing the ugly duckling meets Alan Partridge song again.

Becca and I have lunch at the home of a family with a severely handicapped 8-year-old who needs to be spoon fed and carried. They are brilliant. It must be hard for them. If I have children I pray they are healthy. Where did that thought come from?

May 15

Building work has begun next door to the church on the next empty plot. Many skylarks have been made homeless at a cruel time of year. A former building society, now a bank, is relocating its call centre there. Jobs for the youth group?

May 16

Today I am awoken by a bleeding paper boy (no, really). Harry had fallen over on his paper round and cut his eye. Since Harry's parents have no car I phone them and offer to take him to hospital. He and I have the delightful privilege of a deserted Accident and Emergency Unit and the undivided attention of a doctor, sister and two nurses. Nothing broken and not even a stitch needed. 'It's a head injury,' says the impressive doctor. He asks Harry if he has any memory loss. When Harry responds in the negative the doctor follows up with, 'Who killed Egmont IV?'

'I can't remember,' says Harry, falling right into his hands. Good to know the health service has a sense of humour. After treatment, we have to fill in a questionnaire about the standard of service we have received.

May 17

GCSEs begin. I have issued an open invitation to tea in the youth room from 4–6 pm to anyone who wants to chill after exams. Proves popular.

May 18

The bishop has invited all the diocese's youth workers to lunch. It must be terrible being a bishop. He and his wife live in a palatial house which many of us are wandering around. Later on the bishop's wife walks into the room and I stand politely to greet her. She sits me down again and explains it is unnecessary to rise when she enters the room. Later on still I am joined by two male colleagues. The bishop's wife again enters the room. They both stand up and I don't. She tells them not to bother and they look daggers at me because I didn't.

The bishop is good company and genuinely interested in what we are doing and our problems. Most of us have short-term contracts, no pension and I am one of the few who feels he is treated reasonably by his employing church. The meal is not unlike that experienced on what politicians call the plastic chicken circuit, but satisfying enough.

The bishop has a big event that evening for people who might give the diocese a lot of money. He asks for help setting up a PA. By the middle of the afternoon, I am being described as the PA expert, even though my advice, that behind a flower arrangement is not the best place for a loudspeaker, is not heeded. Never confuse lack of ignorance with expertise.

Our five-a-side team finally plays its first, second and third matches, winning two and drawing the other 1-1. I score both goals in the draw, which makes the lads from our church very happy. They claim to have the own goal on video.

May 19

If you are ironing and the iron overbalances, and you have good reactions, don't try to catch it. I was, and it did and I did and it hurts. Perhaps God is trying to stop me doing housework on my day off.

May 21

After playing too much quiet stuff in church, we turn up the volume for a bit after the service but are told to be quiet by people praying in the side chapel. I stop and they say that I didn't need to stop, only play quieter. My comment, 'You can't move the drums and we've prepared a loud piece', does not lead to an offer from them to move somewhere else to pray.

May 22

Unusually for a Monday, I do a weekly shop round the supermarket. It's not as busy, but they don't seem to have so much stuff to sell. I also take about three times longer than usual because it is the time when most of the church's retired people do their shopping. They all say things such as, 'Aren't you lucky being able to shop during the day.' They say it in a semi-accusing way, or is that just the way I hear it? I have done two hours at my desk before I come out, have a lunchtime Christian Union meeting to speak at, then a staff meeting and the Youth Committee meeting tonight. I expect by the time I get to bed I will have done ten hours work. Sometimes I hate this job. They are lucky to be able to shop during the day. They live in a country where the life expectancy means you can retire.

Pondering on this, I decide to take action. In future, I will agree with people who seem to be accusing me of not working during the day. I will say, 'Yes it's great only having to work on a Sunday,' or some such guff.

May 23

A visit to the Christian Resources Exhibition in London with the staff team. My friends Kate and Rick (recently married; still smiling all the time) have challenged me to bring back the tackiest bit of Christian fringe material I can. Last year it was the 'Christians in Carpets' brochure. I wonder what this year will have in store?

A quick look round shows me that the tackiest item on sale is Baptist Union Rock at 50p a stick. It's going to be a very hard act to beat.

I buy some Bible study resources, books, new drumsticks and have a bag of catalogues the size of Scandinavia.

The key question addressed by the exhibition is, 'When two or three are gathered in Jesus' name what will they sit on?'

May 24

The day after the exhibition I am completely drained of all human resources like strength and stamina. I do virtually nothing useful all day. I finish reading the book I've wanted for ages (less than 24 hours it took), by a humanist Christian minister, thrown out of his job for not believing in a God 'out there'. I thought I'd find a lot of points of connection between his book and my thoughts, but ended up dissatisfied. How can he say he still feels 'called' into the ministry? Who called him?

May 25

Remember that I haven't checked my email for a few days. It runs to 28 messages, of which 25 don't need to be responded to or kept.

Two five-a-side games. Win one and, gasp, lose one.

May 26

First pee of the morning feels like passing razor blades. Drink a gallon of water and try again. Only slightly better. Do something I never do which is by-pass the system and phone a doctor friend. He says I have either got an STD or urethritis. I ask what an STD is and discover it isn't standard trunk dialling.

He prescribes me some antibiotics. If I have an STD I will be the world's unluckiest man. If I'm going to have the TD I might at least start by having the S.

I think I have also got respite-lessening disorder – I only seem to get ill on my day off.

May 28

The deep joy of a painless pee fills me with excitement for a Sunday's work. Brian are cool and the sermon in the evening service by a guest from a missionary society is genuinely helpful.

May 29

At the staff meeting, I learn that Pete has accepted a curacy and will be moving here. He will be ordained at the end of June. I am delighted to be getting a colleague who looks as if he will be a soul friend.

There is a phone call during the meeting and it is the news that Vernon has died. He has had a heart attack at work. He was 54. He has two sons doing GCSEs and A levels right now. Lots of the teenagers at church know them both well. I think the next few days might be difficult.

The after-GCSE club sits round talking and praying once I have told them about Vernon. They are all shocked. As chair of the Youth Committee, Vernon often said helpful and encouraging things about youth work during church services, so the kids really respected him. He was good at talking to young people as well.

Youth Committee will need a chair. Can't think of anyone. Too early.

May 30

Funeral has been set for next Tuesday. I call round to see the family. Can't think of anything to say but they are brilliant and grateful and sad all at the same time.

Questions for May

1 Trudge seems to condone a lot of popular culture and work with it, rather than against it. Do you agree with him?

2 Think about how you use visuals. Are they designed to reinforce the things you really want people to remember?

3 Safety versus expediency again. Right decision?

4 Ring any bells? How do you cope with this?

5 If your team need to have a discussion about the relationship between baptism and confirmation or the place of infant baptism in Christian society this is probably the time to do it.

Barbecues and outreach

June

June 1

Let's talk about anger. I find myself getting really angry with a guy who parks his BMW (soft top) in front of me in the queue for the car wash and then goes to buy a token. I already have a token. I was angry even though:

1 I have just used the same technique myself at the vac station.
2 I have occasionally done this myself.

There is a party in the evening in the church hall (warning – no alcohol at a party, danger, danger). Guests are mainly dressed the way Christians dress and with Christian, shared-meal type food (ie grim). The only saving grace, and it is a slim one because on top of all this there is no music, is that I meet a guy from RoSPA (Royal Society for the Prevention of Accidents). We have a long and interesting conversation about safety aspects on residential youth work. I learn a lot. He explain to me how a lot of the legislation since the Lyme Bay canoe tragedy has caught up many safety-conscious and careful youth leaders who used to do outward bound activities and are now scared to.[1] We reminisce about potholing. Both of us used to do it with young people and now prefer only to go with friends.

June 4

Happiness in ministry is an unexpectedly dull Sunday. Discuss.

June 5

It would have been Youth Committee tonight but it has been cancelled in view of Vernon's death and imminent funeral.

Most of my prayers at the moment are of the, 'Is anybody there?' type. A long chat with Rob over a pint is a help because we spend the time planning some things we will do in the future. He admits that he often feels the way I do at the moment (at least once a week he wakes up not believing in God), but he continues to behave and act as a Christian because he is one.

Not believing in God for a bit shouldn't be allowed to upset your pattern of behaviour.[2] Fascinating insight which I need to go away and deal with. Meantime a prayer:

'Lord, I'm still here if you have anything you want to say to me.'

June 6

Wake up with a desperate need to read Ecclesiastes. I have no idea why apart from last night's prayer and it is my favourite book at the moment. It tells me that people have always tried to make sense of life without God and it isn't easy.

'Words of wisdom are like the stick a farmer uses to make animals move. These sayings come from God, our only shepherd, and they are like nails that fasten things together.' (Ecclesiastes 12:11 – Contemporary English Version)

Vernon's funeral is a delight. He has an unbelievable family of believers who are determined to give thanks for his life. I find it very hard to sing.

The suspicion that summer is around the corner turns into a church hall that's far too hot for the post-funeral bunfight. The hall has air conditioning but people here can't grasp the basic principles and so open the windows letting the outside, hotter air in. Our beautiful, octagonal, glass-roofed hall becomes a greenhouse. Instead of falling out with people at a wake, I leave early to meet the young people and their Bible study group. They are coming to my house today to avoid colliding with the funeral stragglers in the hall. For reasons best known to them, they rifle through my record collection, play a number of fine 80s classics and laugh at them.

We manage a few verses of John's Gospel too.

I have broken a tooth on a piece of granary bread leaving a small chasm. All manner of foodstuffs can gather for a short meeting during each meal after which I spend the next three hours doing excavation with my tongue.

June 7

Another hot day. Bad news for those doing two and a half hours of GCSE maths paper two. I have an appointment with a finance company who may be able to wheedle and wangle a few extra quid without increasing my monthly commitments. We shall see.

Well, yes they can, without costing me any more per month.

I have discovered that small wooden cocktail sticks are excellent for discreetly hacking food out of my cavity without, a) hurting and b) damaging the tooth further.

Post-GCSE group need to chill in more ways than one. One of the girls got told off during the exam for taking too many clothes off. The girls at our local comp don't wear many clothes in summer anyway.

June 8

Five-a-side tournament ends today. It has been contrived that winning the league (which we do) doesn't mean winning the competition. We have to play the second placed team again for that honour. Having thrashed them in a league game 3-0 early in the evening, we lose 1-0 to them in the final due to a dodgy penalty decision. They are young people without any older help so it is a good thing. I keep telling myself this. It is good to have lost. It doesn't sound any better how ever many times I say it. Coming second means you lost better than everybody else.

June 9

Croissants, coffee and two newspapers for breakfast. Get increasingly nervous during the day because I am going to meet Becca's parents. We spend the evening at a nice restaurant. They are a delightful couple, although her father is one of those people who talks louder than I find comfortable in public. People at nearby tables turn to look but he doesn't notice. He pays for the meal, which isn't cheap, so I forgive him. I am happy for others to be the centre of attention as long as they are prepared to fund it.

June 10

Youth group and Brian joint barbecue. They have been encouraged to bring their friends. I bring Becca and a guy I know from the gym I don't go to often enough. It was hard to persuade him to come but I try and make myself do the difficult things I ask the kids in the group to do. I am doing a ten-minute challenging talk after the food.

Lots of the kids have brought friends, which is brilliant. Jo has brought her mum.

The thing our youth team does absolutely best is eating. It is like opening a door into an area of expertise. People who are hesitant about leading prayers or Bible studies can cook sausages for England.

Since it has been on my mind, I do my talk from Ecclesiastes, talking about a man who tried to make sense of the world without God in it but couldn't. Lots of good conversations seem to be happening around the glowing barbecue embers as the evening light fades.

June 11

It is the final Sunday for our present curate. It occurs to me that I have said very little about this man and have not even given him a name. How appropriate. He is now an SEP (Someone Else's Problem). The liberal cheque handed over by the vicar as a leaving gift is a sign of the church's relief, not overwhelming generosity. In his farewell speech, the curate thanks the church for all we have taught him. It's mutual. I have heard a number of people leaving meetings with this guy saying, 'Well that's taught me a lesson.'

He never said anything wrong, but, typical of some more fundamental, conservative evangelical clergy, he seems to have had no love for people. I disagreed with everything about him except his words. I once saw some papers on his table about an organisation called 'Essentially Evangelical'. It looked like it was formed out of the creeping realisation that someone in the all-male, heterosexual, moat-builders association had left the drawbridge down.

He always complimented speakers if they were clear, or very clear. Often clear but never interesting. He wore brogues and tucked his shirt into his trousers. Bye.

June 12

The Youth Committee meets, prays and appoints Clive as chair. Since he never has anything to say about youth work but is well organised he may well turn out to be perfect. We then list a few people we'd like to co-opt (get to join) on to the committee to make up the numbers. Someone suggests we ask a couple of young people. I suggested this myself a few months back and it was pooh-poohed. Now it is somebody else's idea it is received warmly. Quickly swallow a humility pill and congratulate the suggester on her brilliant idea.

June 13–15

Apart from various face-to-face youth activities I have put this time aside to prepare for our summer camp. Amazingly it hasn't been too badly whittled down and I get loads of stuff done, including cleaning and making an inventory of all our board games and outdoor gear.[3]

June 16

Wrecked. Am helping with music at a parish wedding tomorrow so try not to drink too much in the evening. Fail.

June 17

I've mentioned that weddings go on for ever and ever now. I also find that I am noticing the details more and more and sort of absent-mindedly planning my own. Here's an exact timetable:

9.55 Leave home. Pick up suit from cleaners.
10.15 Arrive in church, set up and tune up.
10.45 Sing and play for half an hour.
11.30 Service due to start.
11.40 Bride arrives.
12.30 Break down gear. Bride and groom greet people at the door (nice touch – not everyone is going to the reception).
1.30 Head for reception.
1.45 Drink in bar while waiting for reception to start.
2.00 See 1.45.
2.15 Line up to shake hands (again in some cases).
2.30 Meal. Meet groom's brother and surmise that he is probably gay. Is this why his table is so far from the top table?
4.00 Speeches. Best man gives out international result. Git.
5.00 Go home and watch video of international football.

7.45 Travel to evening reception. Ignore barn dancing.
11.15 Bride and groom leave for local hotel.

Thirteen hours plus. I'm determined one day that I will ask the bride and groom, after the honeymoon, if they were too tired for sex.

June 18

When I arrived here, I suggested that the evening service would die if it did not change. The evening congregation is down to about forty people from its previous seventy, and there is little sign of the trend changing.

Until tonight. The whole youth group come in force and increase the numbers back up to sixty. I have told them that if they start to come regularly they will earn the right to have an interest in what happens and to suggest changes.

After the service they look nervous at what they have taken on, but it gives me a chance to ask at tomorrow's staff meeting if I can preach more in the evening. At the youth group meeting, we plan an imaginary evening service. At the suggestion of one of the 14-year-old girls we also pray for all the regular members of the evening congregation who may not like our ideas. Brilliantly wise.

June 19

I ask about preaching more. My vicar says, 'What are you going to do less of? You're already complaining you're too busy.' Didn't expect that. It's terrible when your own wisdom comes back to haunt you. The logical thing to give up is playing drums since it's nothing to do with my job description but simply something I happen to be able to do. But I do it because I enjoy it more than most of the things in my job description. 'I'll have to give that some thought,' I find myself saying.

June 20

John's Gospel studies have reached the feeding miracle in chapter 6 and we have our own fast-food phenomenon by phoning for pizzas.

June 21

Spend most of the day on site at church, tidying up debris from nearby building work which has blown into the churchyard or been thrown into the car park. Did a bit of late spring-cleaning in the youth hall and photocopied the world in readiness for a big, post-exam party praise meeting on Sunday night.

June 22

The vicar has had his car hit in the rear by an AA recovery vehicle. I love irony.

Head to the city centre Christian Bookshop to research books for the camp. End up trying to find books to encourage myself in my Christian life. Buy three. It may not be enough.

June 24

Becca and I drive to a National Trust Garden in Gloucestershire. Have a nice walk round. I enjoy listening to the snatches of conversation of strangers:

'...only likes them cooked once.'

'I said if he ever did that again it had to be red.'

'...don't think Angela meant any harm to the cat but it was a shame.'

I'm a dangerous listener.

We make a list of things that sound like they ought to be shrubs:

Mirage, Agenda, Hysterectomy, Colostomy, Panic, Maniac, Howitzer, Tribunal, Espionage, Formica, Diplomat, Ravage, Dysentery, Ming, Democracy, Anonymous, Malingering, Syphilis.

Becca suggests Trudge. I say she is a smart-arse. 'I've got a nice bum,' she says, 'I'm sure that's what you meant.'

They could also be boys and girls names. 'Come on in, Hysterectomy, your tea's ready.'

We drive over to my folks in the evening. They are not so restauranty as Becca's parents so we are having a meal in with them. Becca impresses them. Knew she would.

June 25

Hay fevered. Becca stopped the night. In the spare room, thank you for asking, although it was a wrench to say goodnight. In the morning, she brings me coffee in bed and gets in. Offer to make her breakfast but by the time I have decided what music to play while cooking she has started. I think this annoys her but she doesn't say.

We are more relaxed than usual because we are going to Pete's ordination at the cathedral and the service starts later than our normal morning service. Plus, we have reserved seats.

It is a lot more prancing around but the bishop is good value. I am moved by the reading from Romans 12, '...be transformed by the renewing of your mind.' Whilst my faith is rocky (as in shaky, not rock-like) at the moment, I am spending a lot of time thinking about it. Am I renewing my mind? Or do I need to let God renew my mind. Another of my prayers:

'Lord my mind is yours for renewal if you want it.'

I expected to be laying it on a bit thick at this point but can't find it in myself to be anti-Anglican because the formalities are done so well in this service. If there has to be a certain amount of prancing about in a cathedral service then it is the worst thing in the world to do it apologetically.[4] The 'welcome' at the start of the service is welcoming, especially the news, unusually for a cathedral congregation, that there is a creche and Sunday School. In the service, the drama, acoustics and colour are powerful. It is loud, ceremonial and yet sensitive to individuals – the families of the candidates are invited to leave first so they can offer their greetings before the mob arrives.

Later a post-exam praise party – an evening of thanksgiving for the end of exams. It is a wonderful mixture of the seriously profound and great laughs which the kids have dreamed up themselves. Their award ceremony for various things is so funny I nearly stop breathing.

Emma wins an award for the best essay written whilst stripping.

Jon is awarded for best nose bleed in maths 1.

Then they give me an award for best non-parental support during examinations. Never got wind of that. It is a meal out for two at the local wine bar and they tell me I have to propose while I'm there. Manipulative toads. Decide to take Rob not Becca.

June 26

At the staff meeting I suggest giving up drums. Vicar suggests I still play occasionally to keep my hand in. Good compromise.

Our church has a 'motto' ever year. We play around with some ideas for next year. The vicar wants it to be 'Let your light shine'. All I can tell you, after an hour's discussion, is that it is an anagram of 'I'll try to shine huge', which I prefer but apparently our mottos are always biblical. So?

June 27

Pete calls round for a meal and to borrow some painting equipment. We talk as if we have known each other for years.

June 28

One of the youth leaders works in a design office and has permission for me to go there to prepare some visual material for the camp. Sometimes offices are a real constraint to creativity. In the open-plan office there are 16 people. Everyone except me apparently has an ability to get their head down and block out interruptions but I am regularly interrupted by people offering me coffee and checking I am OK. Then, when the news gets out that I work at the church I spend the rest of the day doing apologetics. Still I get three names to contact when we do our next evangelism course.

Sadly I don't seem to generate very much creative oomph and have more hay fever. I return a little depressed.

June 29

There is a pile of stuff waiting for me at home (in tray and email).

In the kitchen area at church I meet Richard, from the Technical College. I introduce myself and he tells me it is his last day. He has been on work experience in the parish for a week. Have I been around that little?

June 30

Today's day-off illness is a hay-fever-based cough.

Questions for June

1 Take a moment to consider the next youth event you are running. Have you done a safety check or risk assessment?

2 At what point does doubt become unbelief and, more seriously, at what point on this spectrum should someone in Christian ministry resign?

3 Do you find that ring-fencing time in your diary works or does it get 'whittled away'?

4 Where do you stand on things 'ceremonial'? Good thing or not? What about symbolic acts, and what is the difference?

Camps and houseparties

July

July 1

A youth worker in a nearby church, Dave, has asked if we can chat. I don't know him very well but I seem to be taking on the mantle of the old and wizened youth worker having done two and a half jobs (the half if you count my gap year doing youth work). Dave's church is interesting. Their youth group trip this weekend is an opportunity to go flying. They recently took their group to visit the Normandy war graves.

Dave is having a lot of difficulty because he is objecting to some of the tasks the church are wanting him to do, many of which seem to be more the role of a caretaker than a youth leader. Having closed up his open youth club and got home at 10.45 pm the other night, he was required to be in at 8.00 am for prayers and then put chairs away in the hall following a private booking.

This guy's employers are a bit sharp, taking advantage of a small line in his job description which expects him to do, 'such other tasks as the minister and deacons may require' but he really ought to pull himself together, smile sweetly and be a Christian not a trade unionist. I don't say this. I am too slow to condemn sometimes – like an exorcist with a stutter. I tell Dave about the association/union for church youth workers and invite him to a retreat I am going to for full-time youth workers. I signed up only a few weeks ago when I saw the publicity advertising it as '... the only training event that expects people to arrive drained and unprepared.' It is very close to the start of my camp but I reckon it will do me more good to arrive at the camp refreshed.[1]

I hope there are spare places.

July 3

I need to get to grips with a task that always gets left until too late – our camp talk scheme. Our team take ages getting round to telling us they are coming then moan that they get short notice of their talks. I like doing the scheme but don't like phoning people. I don't mind being phoned but hate making phone calls. I think it is because I hate being wrong and don't like trying to work out who I am talking to when the phone is answered. If I manage to get all the team's mobile numbers this year the job will be more straightforward next. At least with a mobile you get the person you are calling all the time and don't mistake them for another family member.

How hard am I making it sound to give someone a ring? In one hour of early evening, I get in touch with 15 of the 19 people I need to speak to. All are civil.

July 4

Our youth Bible study group is still plodding through John's Gospel, but enjoying it so plod is the wrong word. During our prayer time, the phone rings while we are praying specifically for further team members on our camp and it is a member of the team confirming that he can now attend. Reminds me of the bit in Acts 12 where the early church are praying hard for Peter to be released from jail but when he turns up at the door they don't believe the servant girl who brings the news. If we only prayed like we were convinced maybe we'd see more answers.[2]

July 5

I've been told that shampoo is unnecessary. All you need do is rinse your hair in warm water and after eight weeks the natural oils start to balance. I'm going to try it over the summer, starting now.

July 6

Polish off the last few phone calls about talks on our camp. Our bookings are up to 125 young people and we have a team of 35. Most of the regular team are coming so I can look forward to ten days of amazing creativity, plus tiredness if I don't pace myself.

Go swimming with a group of Brian lads. Get wet.

July 7

Day off. Hair very greasy. Wear baseball cap all day.

July 8

The party invitation specifies arrivals beginning with the letter p. I wear a pink T-shirt and panama, with a pair of shoes, trousers and sunglasses, plus some pants. In my pocket are a peg, pin, pen, paracetamol, plug, Plasticine, pliers and potato. I carry the letter p section of my record collection. I am deemed the winner until someone arrives at 11.30 pm wearing pyjamas and carrying a pavlova. Apparently he changed in the car on the way back from a concert.

Becca wears a black cocktail dress and an amazingly high pair of heels. When I ask how this fits with the letter p theme, she says, 'You're about to tell me I look perfect.'

July 9

The trouble with good parties where you don't get drunk but do drink all night is that the next day the world feels bad. I can't specifically put my finger on where I feel ill. My stomach is churning, my guts are rotting, my head is aching and it's a Sunday. I try drinking a lot of water then eating a cooked breakfast. I make some progress with a wash followed by more water but I don't fully wake up until the third hymn.

Church isn't as exciting as the party.

July 10

The start of the training retreat for full-time youth workers. Dave is coming and we share transport. We will be staying at a former monastery.

At a pub on the way, the landlady clearly feels that one of these two statements is a joke:

1 Can we have two receipts so we can claim twice.

2 Don't worry, we were joking, we're missionaries.

Unfortunately she believes the wrong one and gives us an inflated receipt.

The retreat has a unique atmosphere. Many of us do arrive knackered, but are rebuilt over the next few days. The guy leading it is friendly enough but tries a bit too hard to be witty and ends up being annoying.

In an excellent opening session, we all think about seeing our lives as either a machine, a battle or a garden. Mine is a garden full of weeds and rocks.

July 11

One guy arrived late last night but no food was saved for him. When one of the leaders asked for some ingredients to make him a sandwich, they were refused. The guy had to go out for a pub meal so we went with him. Only seemed fair.

The day starts with an interesting Bible study on John 21 – funny how John's Gospel is following me around.

The food portions are pretty small but I manage not to buy too much chocolate. I stay up late playing a board game.

July 12

It is a very wet day. I throw myself into the day and chatting/mixing. It is all going very well. This time last year I seem to remember bringing my computer with me and working on something or other during the free time. This year I am pretty free during the free time. I don't manage to read as much as I would like, but still enjoy the retreat.

An exercise where different people all describe the same event in one hundred words and then read their descriptions to each other proves gobsmacking. People were visibly shaken at how many different ways there are to see the same event.[3]

July 13

The end of the retreat. The journey home is interesting. Not being bothered to look at a map, and knowing the direction is vaguely south, we navigate home using the sun as a guide. I like Dave. Maybe I only like people once I have spent time with them. Most of the local people in St Mary's are very suspicious of outsiders. Could it be I am getting that way too?

Our diocesan synod is having a debate about youth work and they've invited full-timers to attend if we want. Decide to. The actual debate isn't one. Nobody speaks against the motion and a number of amendments, designed to sharpen up the motion, fail. That is good, because if they had succeeded the main motion would probably have fallen, along with all the work that has gone into a report recommending investment in youth ministry in the diocese. Anybody out there who understands politics will understand this paragraph. The rest of you (including me) needn't worry. God has created some people to be interested in this stuff. The motion is passed so hooray, the diocese is going to think more carefully about youth ministry in the future and maybe throw a bit of money at it. One clergyman I spoke to said that for the motion to fail, or be spoken against, would be like the Church voting to strangle kittens.

I'd better have a go at explaining synodical government, which will be a challenge. The Church of England is part of one holy, apostolic, catholic and democratic church. Every five years, each diocese elects various clergy (people such as vicars) and lay ('ordinary' people) members to General Synod. Each diocese has its own diocesan synod and each deanery (group of a few parishes) has its own deanery synod. General Synod can pass matters down the line for discussion, the lower synods can pass motions (oops) and ask the higher synods to discuss them. In practice these synods attract people who like committee meetings and church politics and the vast majority of people in the church let them get on with it. The fact is that the choice of vicars is barely democratic and most people in the church are not at all democratic, voting with their feet if some change happens which they do not like, such as removing pews or changing the style of worship. For me, true democracy involves the minority who are outvoted being willing to go along with the opinions of the majority if they cannot persuade them by argument.[4]

July 14

For the first time in recent memory, I arrive at my day off without needing to rest. Clean the house. Then I need to rest.

July 15

Becca and I read sitting on a rug in a country park for most of the day. I have some cricket commentary on which I always find more interesting than actually watching cricket.

I write my two venture talks and prepare Brian for tomorrow. Rest of the time I watch Becca sunbathe.

July 16

Two new members of Brian ask why it has such a strange name. We have a discussion about it and the kids admit that they don't like it either but they never thought I'd go along with their suggestion. We decide to have a proper discussion next term about changing it again.

Everyone says Pete's first sermon is a belter so I make a point of getting hold of the tape. A nice guy who can preach. Wow. How rare is that?

End the morning taking nice woman called Olive to Casualty following the over-zealous plunging of a cafetière during the after-church coffee. Her arm is badly scalded. I don't think our risk assessments covered that. It probably covered everything except reality. It's Titanic planning – very scientific and anticipates everything except what happens.

Listen to the sermon in the car whilst Olive is being treated. It is an excellent talk. He uses his own life story to illustrate the text, but he keeps to the text. The opening line, 'When I was last in prison…' gets everyone's attention instantly. Even on tape you can hear the whole church perk up. He used to be a volunteer prison visitor.

July 17

Last staff meeting until September. Vicar is walking around whistling 'Lord of the Dance'. I do need to get out of this place for a while.

Everyone except the vicar, who is not the world's greatest preacher, thinks Pete's sermon was superb. The vicar thinks it wasn't practical enough.

At my dentists later, I am shown a colour picture of my broken tooth. It looks disgusting. A temporary stopping is put in.

July 18

We spend another day in Rob's garage sorting out the camp equipment. We have a list that, were it ever to fall into enemy hands, would leave them wondering what on earth we were up to. To start with it is called 'The Infantry'. A taster:

8 buckets
2 hoses
6 sharp knives
2 bells
4 balls of string
1 bullhorn
50 sponges
200 balloons
3 baseball bats

If you've never played Whomping the Schnurd or Volley the Splogg you will have no idea what we're up to. The knives (Rob says, 'Put them in the juggling box.') are for the kitchen.

We then spend a happy afternoon shopping for new games and raiding junk shops for drama props, old golf balls and things that might become games. Our campsite is a large public school in Wales with its own golf course.

July 19

At the last young people's get together for a few weeks, I check that the ones going on the camp are organised and know about their train times. I cannot travel with them because we need a two-day advance party to turn a huge school into a summer camp. Two of the fringe lads who I have given up recruiting for the camp ask if there are still places. Of course there are and they are reserved for fringe Christians like them who make their minds up at the last minute.[5]

I have to admit that I have done little young people's evangelism this year so far but most of my energy in the first half of the year is usually reserved for recruiting people to camp. Evangelism is easier there.[6]

July 20

Have a half-day off to do my own washing, packing and preparation. Spend half an hour on the phone to Becca (who is also coming on the camp for the first time) reassuring her that she will be brilliant.

July 21

Rob and I plus two of the camp team load the van we are taking. All the equipment, now carefully sorted and listed, to run a youth holiday for one hundred plus teenagers needs to be taken.

July 22

We travel, on one of the hottest days of the year so far, via a school that lends us a drum kit and a bookshop that sells us books on sale or return. We need to go north and west avoiding the M5/M6 junction on a summer Saturday. Not easy.

We arrive hot and shattered. It feels good to be going to camp, especially because it is a houseparty-type camp, so we get beds and showers. The pre-camp routine involves a meet-up at a pub and then a wander slowly down to the school to set up. The first problem we encounter is a perennial one – tiny flies in the smoke detectors, which set off the fire alarms. We get loads of stuff shifted and most of the school staff leave site, leaving us to be disturbed by fire alarms and with hardly anyone to ask if we need anything.

July 23

We use today as a training day. We enjoy a beautiful, sunny day, with people we have got to know well. We rehearse our jobs, pray, assess risks, have a Bible study, share communion and then have a barbecue together, a cricket match in the background. Idyllic. We always have to keep reminding ourselves that the holiday is about the young people.

July 24

Today the camp starts officially. The day is spent setting up bookstalls, PA, notice boards, a welcome desk and getting ready to be nice. We smarm around parents delivering their offspring, because generally they are the ones who have paid the money. Suddenly, the 40 people on site becomes 160.

July 25

We have our second, night-time fire alarm. Including one on the team weekend, it is the third night out of four I have been up in the middle of the night. Under 'hobbies' I once put on a job application, 'Walking around boarding schools in the dark'. I seem to spend a lot of my life doing it.

We have games of football, crocker (non-stop cricket with a football) and water-balloon volleyball (the previously mentioned Volley the Splogg).

We introduce a smutometer after one particularly crude, lunch-time notice.

Another sunny and uneventful day leads to good conversations, good happenings and a great atmosphere.

The school do not seem to be able to agree on where we should play; one person telling us off for playing where someone else had specifically told us to play. There is frustration in the school that the groundsman is going slightly bonkers.

July 26

Two of the lads in my small dormitory group want to talk about gap years. We grab mid-morning coffee and biscuits together and sit in the sun talking until lunch time before cooling down with a dip in the pool. And they call this work?

In the evening, Becca accuses me of ignoring her and we have our first semi-row. I guess I forgot to explain how busy the main leaders of these things can get. We agree to spend Friday together, missing the trip to a theme park. It is my fault for being so concerned to brief Becca about the work I forgot to explain we might have to put our relationship on hold during the camp.

No false fire alarms tonight.

July 27

Our late-night (well, 9.30 pm) entertainment consists of a monologue by an eccentric ex-army type stranded on a desert island. He is dressed in most of the contents of the drama props box and only the plastic gun gives it a military ring. During this, people keep interrupting to give notices, play games and even advertise one of Saturday's meetings. I think you had to be there. Can't type this without laughing.

July 28

Whilst we had agreed to spend the day together we hadn't said what we would do and so the morning is spent doing some emergency shopping for the cooks. The afternoon is spent asleep by a lake.

July 29

A wonderful Saturday on site. There are games everywhere. The fields and lawns at the back of the school are all full of activity, from juggling to croquet, ultimate frisbee (a most knackering game) to five-a-side football. The swimming pool is also full of activity. I managed 20 lengths last Sunday, 22 on Wednesday and 24 today. An outdoor pool on a hot, sunny day is a nice way to keep fit. Nicer than our local baths on a cold December morning anyway. The last time I tried swimming as a fitness regime, I lasted seven weeks.

July 30

Traditionally, and as an Anglican all that means is that we've done it once before, we have a lie-in on a Sunday. We have a morning service which is over in 50 minutes (excellent Clair, well done) including a chorus done in sign language for the deaf.

After Sunday lunch – well done cooks, roast chicken dinner for almost 200 (we've swollen in numbers due to weekend visitors) is not easy – we wander down to the lake and play frisbee, eat ice-cream and get caught in the rain.

July 31

I only manage ten lengths today before a swimming gala gets in the way. The last full day of the venture is not so warm as it might have been so the gala/party then deteriorates and closes early. This after a pretty successful barbecue in the sunshine. I often pray about the weather and then find myself amazed that it works out as we want. The rain happens at the precise time we want all the young people indoors tidying their dormitories and packing their cases. Brilliant.

This camp has been free from discipline problems. It may simply be that everyone is very nice and well behaved. There are high spirits but no mischief.

At the end we count our progress in a few ways:

Number of known conversions	3
Number of definite re-commitments	8
Book sales	£345 (disappointing)
Damage to school property	£200 (one table-tennis table)
Number coming back next year	100%
Number of evangelistic booklets taken	27
Serious accidents	0 (hooray!)[7]

Questions for July

1 Whose opinion do you agree with, Dave's or Trudge's?

2 Well? What is the relationships between faith and answered prayer?

3 Try this. Each member of your team describes a recent event you have all been part of. They must use only 100 words. Share results and listen to the variety.

4 Are you a political animal, happy to give time to meetings designed to help the wider church run more smoothly? Should more youth workers try to get involved in church government?

5 However full you are at an event, can you make space for non-Christians? The answer should always be 'yes'.

6 Do you agree with this strategy?

7 How do you gauge the effectiveness of residential work? What else could you count?

Holidays
August

August 1

Today is the last day of the camp. We need to clear up, pack up and take our van home. Some of the equipment is staying for another team, some is leaving and likewise the leaders. As it happens, the hand over is not too bad and the 'bitter end' is not really as bitter as it has been in the past. That said, it is painful when I am hit on the shin by a 10 lb tin of plum tomatoes on opening the van door back at Rob's garage.

August 2

Address lists to be updated and my post to be read and sorted. I start a list of things to do but it gets too depressing.

I have an appointment back at the dentists to have a root treatment. Considering what is being done – whanging around in my gums with needles and metal probes – it hurts surprisingly little. However, for the first half of the afternoon I find I am writing things I can't pronounce.

August 3

Today I have enough energy to get a lot of my in tray emptied. Not sure where I put it though.

August 4

Holidays tomorrow. Wash all my clothes. I used to take my holidays outside school holidays as I don't have school-age children and anyway it's cheaper. Sometime in the last few months, I agreed to go on holiday with Becca. How did that happen? As a teacher, she needs to go away in the school holidays.

August 5

Becca and I drive slowly up to the north-west where we have rented a cottage for a fortnight. It is a fantastic place, clearly fitting the geography of my ideal retreat: 'Go to nowhere and turn left'. Nobody has heard of the village we are staying in, it's not even on our map. The local shopkeeper directs us down a dirt track. We come across a church and beyond it we turn right into a field, then cross a cattle grid into another field. In the middle of this second field is a copse with two white stone pillars fairly central. These turn out to be the entrance to the cottage.[1]

August 6

We eat breakfast in the garden with a view of nothing but rolling hills and a distant farm. Then we spend an idyllic day at the side of Bassenthwaite Lake, reading and passing the time. Don't go to church but read Sunday papers in the pub instead. Some of the Sunday papers have more supplements than a weight lifter's vitamin bottle. They will have to be finished tomorrow, on the beach.

August 7

Another great day. All our teas are 'nice cups of' and all our food is 'yummy'. Becca only talks about two types of food – 'yummy' or 'horrid'.

The drive to the nearest road is beautiful, even if we are taking the rubbish out (you have to drive the rubbish to the road). Butterflies chase the car like seagulls chase cross-channel ferries. Cows lazily block the route and have to be 'nudged' away.

The beach is lovely.

August 8

The gap between pressing the green button on 'Pay and Display' car park ticket machines and the ticket being dispensed is long enough to be disconcerting. This has nothing to do with today – the car park incident occurred yesterday but my mind only just noticed. Holidays help that sort of thing to happen.

August 9

On holidays, the worst decision to have to make is whether to drink Dent Aviator or Coniston Bluebird. Or both.

August 10

Almost relaxed now. Writing less and less. Proper holidays. We found this cottage at a fairly late stage. It is attached to the owners' house and in their grounds, which includes a forest (OK copse) and large lawns. The grounds are still very open to nature – grass not cut too short. If it gets too long it looks as if they get some sheep in. The owners have three children aged 9, 6 and 4. The grounds must be a fabulous place to grow up. There is a hammock slung between two trees (an excellent place to sit and think or, on holiday, merely sit), a swing suspended from one tree and a tyre hanging from another, a lawn big enough for a game of football, a large drive to ride bikes up and down... I could go on but the picture is complete enough. The garden is sufficiently planted/cultivated/managed to make it obvious that it is a garden, but left wild enough to attract wildlife. Unless they inherited the place, it must cost the owners a fortune. One of my biggest sadnesses is the amount of money I could have earned if I had not decided on a career in youth ministry.[2]

August 11

A game of 'I spy' in a local town on a wet Friday afternoon becomes lavatorial very quickly. Becca didn't get my '... something beginning with LCIAFFOC'. Well it was 'Lonely Crow In A Field Full Of Cows'.

We try and avoid watching TV every night so we play Monopoly. We manage a proper, full game and she wins in under two hours. I'm a good loser so that's OK; I'm a rubbish winner.

August 12

We found a beach where you can drive right up to the water. When I hit the beach, I tend to hit it hard and move in to stay.

I enjoy the papers, a spy novel and a game of beach cricket with two 12-

year-old boys whose parents are ignoring them. Once a youth worker... Becca is an unbelievable wicketkeeper. I think this swings it and I decide to propose. Soon.

August 13

The male owner of our holiday home is the preacher at the local BCP 1928 HC. (Book of Common Prayer revised 1928 Holy Communion). The Rector is Rev B Strange. Honestly.

They manage to cram a baptism, Holy Communion, twenty minute sermon and five hymns into 75 minutes. Impressive going. The sermon is a bit, 'The trouble with the nation'-y but is interesting enough. I end up feeling like Loyd Grossman must feel after Masterchef – he has eaten well but hasn't had a meal.

I try to think of the best alternative to the song 'Three lions on a shirt'. How about:

Three shirts on a lion
Three lines on a shirt
Sea lions on a shirt

No Monopoly tonight so I give Becca a sound thrashing (at cards).

August 14

Disappointingly we pick a pub from the *Good Pub Guide* and drive a long way to it only to find that Monday night is the chef's night off. I'll write to the Guide. We have a drink there, whilst reading back copies of Hello Magazine and overhearing loud conversations in dialect at the bar (guess the locals all turn out on a Monday night because there are no *Good Pub Guide* travellers around).

We buy takeaway pizza. Yummy, to coin a phrase.

August 15

A day off from beaches to see what Kendal is like. Good charity shops. Home early to enjoy sitting in the garden.

August 18

Last day of holidays, therefore last day at the beach. I try to breathe in the atmosphere and capture it for the next few months. It is good to sit in a stuffy office and recall the sea, re-smell the air and hear the quiet penetrated only by children playing. As I type up these hand-written notes in a stuffy study some weeks later, I do exactly that.

One last fill of idyllic countryside, tea on the lawn and buzzards circling and climbing into the warm hazy sky.

August 19

Uneventful drive home, helped by Becca warning me about a car turning right in front of me which I don't notice.

Home by early afternoon and the washing machine ends its holiday – it'll need sedatives by tomorrow morning.

Derby's season begins with a home defeat.

Last day off work. I've had a great time but I'm not relaxed. To put it in specifically Christian terms, I have no peace. I do know what I want but I don't know how to get there. I have no savings – in fact I have debt. I am not wholeheartedly committed to my job and may need a change. Christian leadership is the wrong place for me at the moment, although I doubt if anyone else will notice that I am teaching people things I don't really believe with all my heart. Inheritance would help but much as I get frustrated by them I don't wish my parents dead. I would love to be in a church where there is consistent, biblical teaching. I need something to get my teeth into.

I also need to talk to the bank but I can't bring myself to do it before Monday. I see it as work you see.

After six weeks of bad hair days, things seem to be getting better and I can almost believe it is true that if you don't wash your hair in anything but warm water for six to eight weeks your hair recovers a natural look.

During a walk in the park later, I bump into one or two of the 18-year-olds from church and find out that some of their A levels haven't gone as well as everyone expected. Some of them have difficult decisions ahead.

August 20

Back to church. If motivation is governed by a little bloke somewhere in my brain, then he still has his deckchair out and his hanky on his head. Pass the time of day with old people. Always good for the youth worker to talk to old people. They need to like you (and pray for you).[3]

August 21

Day in the study. I deal with the bare minimum of stuff and make a loose plan for the week. Play minesweeper on the computer most of the day.

My dear friend (well no, but we have seen a lot of each other recently) the dentist, hacks the temporary filling out of my mouth, whams a few sharp things up into my roots without the aid of anaesthetic, and pronounces the tooth clear from infection and indeed life. He hopelessly underestimates the amount of amalgam needed to fill the enormous hole he's made and eventually charges me a huge amount for the privilege.

He drives a BMW with a personalised registration.

August 22

Get some more work done. Write an article. Produce a training brochure. Write some letters.

Pete has an open house tonight so I pop in for tea. Everyone else pops out as I arrive, but I'm not paranoid.

The evening sees a meeting of our youth Bible Study group, informally for August. Four more people than usual turn up (making 11 altogether), including two non-Christian friends of regular members. Becca pops in later. Every time she walks in these days, the girls look at her engagement ring finger and then give me harsh stares.

August 23

GCSE results. All of our kids have done what they expected and can go on to sixth form if they want to.[4]

Two friends invite Becca and me for dinner. Last time we went it was very formal so we dress up, only to find that we are the only ones looking smart and the meal is to be eaten round the kitchen table.

At not too late an hour, the host says loudly, 'Isn't it time we kicked these good people out if we're going to get to Yorkshire tomorrow?' I enquire if they have an early start and discover it is 10.30 am that they have to leave. So they want us out eh? I'm still not paranoid.

August 26

I do the following exciting things:

repair an extension lead that had stopped working;
empty the ironing basket;
clean, vacuum and fill the car up with petrol;
make two lasagnes;
turn off the bathroom radiator;
watch England throw away another test match.

August 27

I'm settling down to listen to Pete preach live for the first time when there is an SOS message from the youth rooms. There are seven of Brian sitting alone in the room, waiting for a leader to turn up. I go and do my secondary RE lesson (I only have one) on 'What is truth?'[5] Later, I discover that they weren't supposed to go out of church at all today but Pete didn't know that and failed to announce it. I am in charge of this so it is my fault.

August 28

There's a flood in the bathroom and on the lounge ceiling a grey stain has appeared. There's a strange sound of rushing water in the house and the radiator that has started leaking is the one I turned off last night to see if it was causing the rushing sound. Turning it back on again stops the leak and the carpet isn't too badly damaged.

August 29

Do people talk to you? I mean do strangers talk to you? I only ask because I am always being stopped by strangers and asked things. Take this morning for instance. My car needs a service and the garage is a couple of miles from home so I decide to walk. Ten minutes into the walk a person coming the opposite way asks me the time. Five minutes later a lorry pulls up and the driver asks me where Clarence Street is (I haven't a clue).

It is good to be available. If you have a pastoral ministry of any sort, take every opportunity to bump into people. Don't have a paper delivered but go and buy one. Go to the pub at the same time each week, even if you only go once a week, and take your glass back. Go to local shops regularly.[6]

August 30

Wait in all day for the Gas Board who don't turn up. At 9.30 pm, they phone to ask if it is OK for them to arrive on Friday. I pin them down to before 11.00 am. Then I remember when they start work – I have to be up and about by 8.00 am on my day off.

August 31

A phone call from Ian, with whom I led a dormitory group at camp. He asks me to preach at his wedding in November, which I am delighted to agree to. I stipulate that it mustn't be on 1 Corinthians 13: 'Love is patient etc, etc.' He says he would never do that because it is the wrong context for the passage. I love him.

What passage shall we have at our wedding?

Questions for August

1 Do you think Trudge should make a point of explaining the sleeping arrangements? Is this the church's business or should it all work on trust? Be honest, do you want to know?

2 Is money an issue for you? If so, how do you address it?

3 Do you think that youth workers tend to miss this essential point – telling the rest of the church what they are up to?

4 Do you make time available to support young people when they get their exam results?

5 Do you have a repertoire of material you can do at very short notice?

6 How good are you at 'putting yourself about' in the community?

Starting over

September

September 1

While waiting for the Gas Board, I manage to do the filing that has piled up in my study. I also go through the tray of correspondence that has piled up in my study and fill the filing tray back up again. There's something wrong with me; I can't convert theoretical work systems into ones that work for me. People say, 'Oh Trudge you're so tidy and organised.' I think they add, in their heads, '… for a youth worker,' but maybe that is my over-sharpened critical awareness.[1] Anyway they should see the cupboards into which I tidy things when people are coming round.

I have a friend who is untidy. His study is a tip. His response to criticism is that he has a very ordered mind and is able to cope with a large amount of superficial disorganisation.

I can also manage a budget for my work of several thousands of pounds but can't pass a CD shop without spending money I haven't got.

The Gas Board arrive at 2.30 pm, a less than creditable effort at coming two days earlier or before 11.00 am. The guy who fixes the leaking radiator tells me it was a gland nut that needed tightening. As if I know what a gland nut is and would be prepared to risk tightening it. The church pays the Gas Board a maintenance charge so I don't have to know what a gland nut is or how to tighten it. Also they are not the Gas Board any more.

September 2

Sarah, our gap-year volunteer, is joining us today. I opt for the relaxed approach to induction.[2] This is good because I haven't had a chance to prepare anything complicated.

She is staying with Maureen, which will, I think, be good for both of them. Maureen is generous and will be understanding of a volunteer on pocket money, but she is also a bit lonely and Sarah comes across as happy to solve that. After having tea with both of them, I leave them to spend the evening together. I first brief Sarah that the vicar will be interviewing her in church tomorrow morning.

September 3

The noise of water rushing through my house is still there, but water isn't rushing out of any overflows and the floors aren't rising up on waves of escaping sewage, so I have no idea what's going on. I really need to find the enthusiasm to phone the Water Board and have someone check all this out. They're not the Water Board any more though.

Reading the church notice sheet, I discover a typing error of awesome proportions in the prayer list. We are meant to be praying for the late Mr Walker's family. The L and the N on a keyboard are not that close together

Sarah interviews well and Mr Walker's family are not in church.

September 4

Sarah is going to do a lot of youth work and I am delighted that this means there will be someone around to be a friend to the girls at the various after-school activities. All the youth team come round to the church rooms for a welcome meal and an autumn term planning meeting.

September 6

A training day I am helping to plan for November 7th is getting nearer. The Archbishop of Canterbury will be addressing full-time youth workers and their clergy. About six months ago someone from the diocese asked if I'd like to help and I had forgotten all about it until the invitation to go to an all-day meeting in London. I take a train to London for a meeting at Church House.

The meeting is chaired by someone who is very good at assuming that others will do the work and then keeping his head down. He is not devious about it. He simply confesses to being full of ideas but not application. Clever. I get more work to do.

Disconcertingly, the luminous destination sign on the return train bears the wrong trip details, but my fellow passengers assure me the train does go to Birmingham. The train shoots through Beaconsfield without stopping, although the sign suggests it should have.

Trains are fun, but they make me nervous.

September 7

Sit down with Sarah to plan how she can best be used over the next few months. I have been a good organiser and teacher but, when I am honest with myself (which is rarely), I have to admit that I don't have that charisma to be in front of a group of young people and make the whole experience feel good for everyone. Sarah has. She is funny, charismatic, confident, reacts well to interruptions and can play the guitar well. She may be the oomph our group needs to take off. Everyone needs a leader to follow and I think the kids will follow her.

Having made the decision to go to the cinema, I am the only person there when the lights go down. Thursday afternoons were never the most popular times with audiences. The escapism of Bruce Willis is what I need to stop my stomach knotting up about all the jobs I am behind with. Also I can't really afford it, but we're talking about staying sane here; I can't afford not to.

In the evening Rob, Trudy and I undertake a review of our summer camp. Rob produces four pints of Scrumpy. Of all the things you could do with apples, why did they choose this one? Headache follows.

September 10

At the start of each academic year, I talk about youth work to all three of our congregations, which means I have the joy of being up for an 8.00 am Holy Communion (Book of Common Prayer). The average age of the congregation at this service is deceased. They look, without exception, like the sort of people who sit staffing rooms in National Trust houses.

I enjoy the discipline of preaching blind on these occasions – making up as sound a sermon as I can on the basis of the readings without seeing them before the service.

Can I talk about youth ministry on the occasion of the Festival of the Blessed Virgin Mary? You bet I can. We need to have a balanced view of Mary if it is to be scriptural. We need to remember that she was young when she conceived – perhaps only a teenager of fourteen. Teenagers can be obedient and they can ponder on God's word. My job is to help them. I am so pleased with this sermon that later I write it down and have another couple of goes at it.

The Sunday evening youth group sees a few new faces (some families have moved in over the summer) and some older Brians joining in. I explain that we are going to be having different meetings every other Sunday from now on – one week in small groups, the next in a bigger celebration-type meeting. The young people, who are often more resistant to change than the staunchest 8 o'clocker, don't seem to get it but I ask them to give it a go for the term.

September 12

In the evening, our Bible-study group reconvenes with another new member (we are growing without trying too hard) and continue our journey through John's Gospel. We have reached chapter eight in nine months – thirteen to go.

September 13

Sarah is the first employee of the church to wear a purple and green rasta hat in the office all day.

September 16

Try to relax but on reading some rubbish in the church press from people who don't understand teenagers, I become compelled to dash off an article.

Becca is going to the hen night of a woman who has left teaching to get married. She has decided to get married because she is pregnant. Angie (for that is her name) is to be found in the exclusivity of Yates' Wine Lodge sporting a hat made of condoms. Bit late for that.

I take a nice bottle of wine round to Rob and Trudy's and tell Becca to join us there later. I enjoy the walk down the High Street on a Saturday night. It is lively and exciting, although not in a threatening way like some places I have lived. The girls are mainly wearing skirts that wouldn't reach the ground if you sawed their legs off. It is a shame that is all they can afford.

We are on our second bottle by the time Becca arrives, and Trudy isn't drinking very fast. Becca smells of smoke. Rob brings in a tray containing a piece of cheese wrapped in plastic, a two kilo tub of marge, a box of crackers and an onion. 'I think presentation skills are really important,' he claims.

Will I be sober enough to walk across town again, devoting my romantic attention to Becca? Will I wake up fresh as a daisy to preach at St Paul's, a nearby church? Can I have one more glass before I go?

September 17

Somehow I was fresh and, as St Paul's has a later start time than we do, I had time for a decent breakfast first as well.

Vergers. What a strange breed they are. I have found them the oddest of all companions over the few years of my ministry, apart from Arthur at my gap-year parish, who was that deadly combination of drunk and personable. We got on fine until one Christmas Eve when he spilled more communion wine than the clergy distributed.

Today's contender is called Bill (I think). When I thank him for moving a table for me he says, 'Don't push it!' Struggling to know what this means and what I have done to upset him I decide to be rude to him all morning with a smile on my face. This works. Most vergers respect clergy, for they give the orders and are deemed important. Act like a clergyman and you will pull it off. When I was at that gap-year parish I once asked the verger to do something and he said, 'Is that what the rector wants us to do?' I said it didn't matter because it was my responsibility and the guy point blank refused to do it until he knew it was the rector's will. From then on I used the phrase, 'I think the rector would like it if…' a lot. It helped. He resigned.

Bill helps me with my microphone. It doesn't amplify my voice but it hangs in a seemly way. He shows me an article which he has written for some vergers' publication, about potatoes not wanting to be cooked. He asks me what I think, so of course I tell him it is wonderful and fits in with my sermon absolutely. He is pleased with this and agrees with me.

Service is hopeless and not only because it is Matins (morning prayer with choral bits). The music is well done but it is for the benefit of 26 elderly folk who don't respond at all to my preaching and say gibberish things to me afterwards.[3]

The vicar invites me to lunch even though I had expressly said that I wanted to get back. He understood whilst looking sad. He is a recent widower and lonely I think, bless him. The afternoon is spoiled by West Brom putting four first-half goals past Derby at the Hawthorns, a game I choose to attend. Draw the second half one all.

The first of the youth group house groups sees three lads and four girls meeting at mine. It starts a bit slowly but then warms up as they cotton on that no one will be expecting right answers just personal opinions of how scripture applies to them. By the end, we are laughing and praying for each other. Think it may be good. I have to play some really terrible music to get them to leave. Jilted John works best.

At 10.00 pm, I try to catch up on the weekend's papers before sleep overcomes me. Whenever I'm trying to finish the papers in a hurry (I hate missing things), I always find them more gripping than ever. Today they are packed full of interesting articles – books well-reviewed, even sculpture I want to see and a fascinating piece about habitable bridges. Maybe I am very tired.

September 18

I email off the article which I wrote on Saturday. It may generate thirty pounds or so.

Apparently, the *Digest* (local newspaper) arranged for ten wallets to be dropped in the various suburbs of the city. In our area eight out of ten were returned, making us one of the most honest places to live.

Anyone out there want to buy a couple of nice calfskin wallets? (It's a joke, Mum.)

September 19

Pop along to a morning run by the diocese, where a new evangelistic programme for use with young people is being launched. The speaker makes the not uncommon mistake of seeing unchurched young people in terms only of sex, drink and drugs. They are not exactly the evils everyone thinks. Most people who drink don't become alcoholics, most drug users try it then stop of their own accord and there is no reason to abstain from sex in the absence of a sound Gospel understanding of relationships.

I sort of bluff my way through the evening study on John 9 which, by God's grace (I think I believe that), teaches us lots and ends up being a real learning experience.

September 20

Opposite the church, the building work is almost finished and some sort of opening ceremony is being planned. There are guys manically planting trees and painting car park lines by arc light. The pretty signs are up, a marquee has a running order on the door but the insides of the buildings don't look at all ready.

Sleep for nine and a half hours, a recent record.

September 21

Today is Ron's funeral. He was a wonderful, Christian man – a little dithery in his last few months but otherwise a snappy 89 years. He was very nice to me when I arrived in town. Also, as an ex-missionary, he lent me a pair of khaki shorts for a sketch when I needed them. He never took himself too seriously but managed to be wise too. The church will miss him. He sometimes came to youth events with cotton wool in his ears. 'I hate it,' he said, 'but I've got to be there.'

September 24

The sermon in church this evening drives me very close to distraction. The preacher ignores the Bible passage and spouts his own thoughts, one of which is blatantly wrong, if you read the passage he is ignoring.

Melinda has lost her wallet with £16 in it. She thinks she left it in a plastic bag at the side of a football pitch where she was watching her brother play. On a whim, I drive her down there whilst Sarah is starting the youth group celebration. Amazingly we find the bag exactly where Melinda had left it and the money is still there. She asks if we can drop by her house to tell her parents, as she had phoned them to say she had lost it before coming to the church.

I wait outside. Ten minutes later she has still not emerged so I knock the door. 'Melinda won't be coming to your church again, Mr Gilbert,' says her Dad. 'Please leave.' As I walk back to the car I hear a knock on a window behind me. At an upstairs bedroom, Melinda is in tears and mouths the word 'sorry'.

September 25

First thing in the morning, the vicar knocks on the door. He has never done this before. He usually calls me and occasionally summons me. I make coffee and we sit down. He has had his ear burned by Melinda's dad who was furious that I took his daughter out alone in the dark. 'Wasn't that a bit of a stupid thing to do?'

I love hindsight. I could do a Masters in it. I explain that I was moved with sympathy for someone and also had an idea (finding her wallet) that needed to be put into action at once. It worked. We found it.

The vicar and I talk for an hour. After we have discussed Melinda, the vicar says that someone saw me going to the cinema last Thursday afternoon and it wasn't my day off. So? I end up in tears, which is more the culmination of lots of different things than this one alone.[4]

He concludes that I am sorry and want to repent. He is surprised when I tell him to leave.

We seem to be reaching a stage in cultural development where you can't offer to help anyone of the opposite sex because you may be a rapist. You can't talk to children you pass in the street because you may be a paedophile. You can't allow your girlfriend to stop the night because people might think you're having sex before marriage. And you can't go to the cinema on a Thursday because it's not your day off. As if the rest of the world only goes to the cinema on a Saturday.

September 26

Can't afford to resign but I want to. Can't conjure up the emotional energy to work. Decide to go the doctors. Phone. As usual he can see me in six days time. Mid-morning I phone Pete. 'Don't move!' is his response. A few minutes later, he is at the door clutching six bottles of Old Peculiar and a takeaway pizza. He phones the school (where I am due in an hour) and tells them I am sick. Then we spend the rest of the day talking, eventually laughing and deciding to stick at it. Pete says the vicar has started on his four-year timetable of sucking the enthusiasm out of his new charges. Pete gives me a well-thumbed book. It is called *How to get things done when you are not the boss*.

September 27

Wake up. Feel OK. Play 'Conditioned Soul' by The Eurythmics very loud. Twice. Scramble eggs and grill bacon. Send Becca text to say I love her. Realise I do. Send Pete a text to say thanks. Send vicar a text to say go stuff your head down the toilet since you are a drain. Remember he hasn't got a mobile. Delete. These are the things that make life worth living. Get text back from Becca. It says, 'Luv?'

Smile through two rescheduled assemblies.

September 28

Plan several 'alternative' events for October and November. Decide to call our alternative Halloween 'Goodbye Ween'.

Go to the cinema in the afternoon again. Film is rubbish but the point had to be made.

September 29

Day off. Receive a copy of a leter from Melinda's father, addressed to the vicar and the diocese. It says, 'I am not happy with the way Mr Gilbert conducts himself, but I am not going to pursue the matter. Melinda has decided to attend the youth club at the Baptist church from now on and will be withdrawn from any school assembly Mr Gilbert leads.'

Don't know whether to laugh or cry.[5]

Sit in a public place in the sun and read a novel. Every time someone from the church passes and makes a comment about it being, 'All right for some!' I agree with them and smile.

September 30

Propose. Accepted. Good.

Questions for September

1 Do you tend to hear criticism even if not explicitly stated?

2 Induction process is really important for newcomers. Do you have one?

3 This is two Sundays running that Trudge has preached to people who have no interest in what he is doing. How useful has this been?

4 So what would you do next? Take a moment to contemplate before reading on.

5 Is this a satisfactory ending? What else could have been done?

Alternatives
October

October 1

I am lunching at the house of the retired managing director of a large company. James is a leading and influential member of our church. His house and grounds are huge. We will be eating venison because his lurcher brought down a deer. He keeps a shot gun in the study, possibly to keep heron off his ornamental fish. He's very nice, hospitable, but awfully 'in charge'.

The agenda – 'I'm awfully concerned that young people don't get anything out of our services' – is heartfelt and I think I've found an unlikely ally in the battle for relevant worship. On a whim, I ask him if he could spare the time to join the Youth Committee. He says he would be delighted. This is one of the few things I can do without asking permission as the Committee is there to support me. As long as it has a PCC representative (which it has) all is well.[1]

James calls me 'Trudge', which is not something all the older members of the congregation manage, but he does it with a look of distaste, as if I am called 'Dogpoo' or something.

When it becomes time to leave I am left in no doubt, courteously, that this is the time.

October 2

I've written some text for the Christmas letter to go out to all the local houses. It's been rejected as too racy. Its not wrong. It's not rude. It's not ill-advised. It is interesting and may set people off reading it. When our church leaders go to a show, I expect they hope the understudies are on. The real performers might be too racy.

A balti meal out with the youth leaders in the evening is a little unsatisfactory. One member of the party comes over all sad and lonely and isolated. Another has a lovely black hair cooked into his chicken. He sends it back saying he is psychologically damaged.

October 3

One of the schools I regularly visit has invited me to be around and sit at a desk for a parents evening, '... to test the water and see if people want to talk to you.' Nobody does but I find it useful to chat to people waiting in a long queue to talk to Mr Johnson about his maths classes. Each parent is allocated five minutes with each teacher but Mr Johnson is running 20 minutes behind after the first three. It may be a long night.

October 5

In a few weeks time, a church, who are running a mission, have challenged us to a youth football match. We have drafted in a few local thugs to augment our minimalist squad, but this evening we have a practice match on the all-weather floodlit pitch at the school. The local thugs take on the old stagers and win 10-5, despite our being 3-2 ahead at half-time. Youth and fitness obviously have a considerable advantage over us. Good job they will be on the same side when the match comes along.

October 8

I'm aware that I have pushed my feelings about the church, and my vicar in particular, to the back of my mind. I do this all the time. I bounce back from bad situations and get on with the job as if nothing has happened. I should confront issues. I have dealt with the whole Melinda thing and I am completely content in my own innocence. I may have been naïve, I may have been a bit hasty, but everything was done out of purity of motive.

Nevertheless, I know that I am arriving at Sundays with no anticipation that I will meet with God and a great desire to avoid the sorts of people who may have complained to the vicar that I went to the cinema on a midweek afternoon.

In the evening celebration, I watch Sarah at work in front of a crowd of young people again. She has certainly got 'it' but I have no idea what 'it' is. I have always argued that you are never too old to be a youth worker but Sarah's relative youth is working in her favour and my thirtysomethingness isn't. Perhaps I try too hard to be liked. After years of trying to do youth work by copying other people who are good, I may have lost touch with who I am.

October 9

I spend a lot of the day listening to old favourite pieces of music. I'm not sure why the urge to do this comes along every now and again. Maybe it acts as a comfort blanket. When I move house I like to get music on in the new place at the earliest possible moment – it reminds me of the way a dog marks its territory by urinating. I play my favourite tracks into the mortar to claim the ground. Or something.

Sometimes my life teeters on the brink of being out of control. Today is clear evidence that it is teetering at an impossible angle because I am going to talk to the Diocesan Evangelical Fellowship (a ghetto of the like-minded) about youth work. Occasionally I wonder if I am held in higher esteem by those outside my own church than in it. The teetering is caused by lack of preparation.

I call in at the home of a newly ordained curate, the son of a former colleague and ex-member of one of my youth groups. It is great to see him enjoying his work, enthusiastic for the gospel and having learned to cook. Nice conversation, nice pasta and a nice walk in the park putting the world to rights. It turns out he knows a guy who has written a very funny book about life in theological college. The book has been slated. That is because the church is the most humourless place on earth and is a sheltering place for those Englanders who have no ability to laugh at themselves.

The evening question and answer session about youth ministry goes reasonably well. I decide that a short and punchy presentation about the purpose of youth work followed by questions is the best way to disguise my lack of preparation. I use Colossians 1:24-29 to make the points that youth work, 'presenting young people perfect in Christ', needs to take seriously:

Prayer
Bible
Gospel
Relationships
Prayer

Or it gets out of balance.

The discussion that follows is lively. A minister, who has been at a previous session of mine, complains that he doesn't know what to do about youth work because they have no young people and nobody in his church likes teenagers. My answer, 'Convert someone who does,' is not appreciated.

October 10

Our evening Bible Study group has ten attendees, a recent record. A sermon was preached at St Mary's last Sunday of the 'you're-all-lukewarm' variety. Some of the kids who are least lukewarm in the world are now repenting. The guy who I most look up to about preaching, says you can probably preach a sermon of rebuke about every four years. I don't think I ever have really. John 10:10 reminds us all that Jesus came that we might have life in all its fullness. If you are following Jesus there's no way you can have a lukewarm life. Good discussion but I can't stop the wrong people feeling guilty.

Halfway through the evening there is a ring on my doorbell and it is Jerry, the guy I met at Spring Harvest, down for the night before Birmingham University open day. He didn't phone to warn me. 'Suppose I'd been out?' I ask. 'You weren't,' he says.

October 11

Up early to get Jerry away for his 9.00 am interview. Discover that shopping at the supermarket is a much nicer experience at 8.30 am than the 5.00 pm rush hour. I am back by 10.00 am, home for my own breakfast as Jerry ate the last of my cornflakes. It is the leftovers of the hunter-killer culture. I went out early, caught my breakfast and now I am enjoying it all the more for that.

Becca and I snatch a few hours together in the evening. The first time we have done so since deciding to get married. We haven't exchanged engagement rings yet and are wondering when to announce it. She says she is going to start coming to St Mary's now but her own church will want to do a proper goodbye when she tells them.

October 12

A letter arrives from two new members of our camp team. They are not happy. What it boils down to, I think, is that our existing team has a very laid-back approach and operates intuitively and flexibly. This helps us to react quickly to the needs of the young people on the camp but means that those who prefer things to be more regimented and planned can get a bit scared. Should I try and become better organised to accommodate the less flexible? Well I know what I want but I think it is what I ought to do that is important.[2]

They say they have no plans to come to the camp again. This means that any alterations we make to our structure will be for the benefit not of them but of others like them. Decide to send a note round the whole team asking for their comments. Unusually for me I do it at once and email it round. Email has made it so easy to communicate. How did we cope before?

October 14

Missionary soccer match. Despite my protests I end up at centre half, a position I have played in only rarely and not for ten years. We go three up pretty quickly and win 7-2. The '2' are both due to errors in the centre of defence in the area I ought to have been in, or was in but inadequately. I enjoyed the after match pint though (once we'd dropped off the under-18s). You can't beat the first 'hit' of beer against post-football throat.

The pub sells Marstons Pedigree. I hadn't noticed how strange the name was until a guy next to me asks the barman for, '... a pint of Pedigree, chum.'

October 15

Today I had one of those preaching accidents that you can't reckon with. In a family service talk I had an illustration which involved throwing an egg up in the air and catching it in a bowl, where it was supposed to smash. Unfortunately it bounced out of the bowl. I threw it up a little higher and it bounced out of the bowl, again without breaking, but then fell a smaller distance onto the aisle carpet where it smashed.

In the evening, we have a multi-media alternative service. It goes well. A band of young people and their mates play instrumental jazz funk before the service. Brilliantly beats organ recitals. Some of the mates aren't Christians and I have wondered about allowing them to be involved before they have a relationship with the God they are helping people to worship. The young people tell me I am too uptight so I relent.[3]

October 16

I return to the church Rob and I visited in the fog in January. It is a pretty part of the world and the autumn wind is hungry for leaves. The church have signed up to send members on the camp next year and I happily spend the morning chatting through youth ministry with the vicar. I say 'chatting through' – he does most of the chatting and I insert the occasional piece of conversational punctuation by asking a question or offering a suggestion. This sends him chattering happily on for several further minutes each time.

October 17

I have a meeting in London and plan to work on the train. Then I meet two colleagues and resign myself to conversation. One of the two has been travelling to the same committee as me on the same line for the last twelve months and I have never bumped into her before. It is also her last meeting because she is going to work in Uganda. The idea of working overseas, which has never bothered me before, bothers me today. Things that make you go 'hmmmm'.

October 22

After the young people's house group, I pop down to the local where the beer is again Marstons. It doesn't taste anything like the gorgeous stuff I drank on Saturday lunchtime. I know I was football thirsty then, but this beer is too cold, too pale and too fizzy. It's hard to manage to get three things wrong with one pint. I think I'll congratulate the landlord. The pub has been modernised to attract the young but it has attracted nobody on this particular night. Actually it has been post-modernised. There is a garage door on the ceiling and random things have been attached to the walls such as golf clubs, old books and strange signs. I particularly like one which says, 'Jesus loves you; everyone else thinks you're a prat.'

October 23

Trying to do some reading and studying. I manage two books today.

Finally understand the difference between baby-boomers (born between the end of the war and the early 60s) and baby-busters (born between the mid-60s and the early 80s and sometimes called 'Xers' – from Generation X). One thesis is that this new generation needs to be evangelised in a new way. The gospel (the good news about Jesus Christ) has in the past been intellectual; the books I read say that Xers need social and emotional content before the intellect gets engaged. Xers want to be friends.

October 24

Our Bible study group continues its plod through John's Gospel and again finds it inspiring and motivating. We've raised Lazarus and now we're wondering how the Mary/perfume incident fits in (John 12). We say farewell to Carol (an assistant leader) who is going off round the world for six months. For some reason it made the discussion of the last part of John 12 a little more lively too; everyone joined in. Talking about Jesus as light of the world is somehow more poignant when someone is about to go and visit a lot of the world.

October 25

I have five days off this week, the consequence of taking insufficient holiday earlier in the holiday year and then trying to cram it all in before Christmas. I feel the need for some other adult company and have reached the conclusion that I am short of the sort of friends who I can call on without an appointment. The youth ministry career path has left my friends spread far and wide round the country.

I need to open up and be honest about the way I feel spiritually at the moment. I'm not sure who to do it with. I'm very self-sufficient and the most likely plan is that I will do nothing about it. That's me folks.

October 30

The bank want to know if I can anticipate my overdraft requirements for the next twelve months. No. Lets go for the lottery ticket and I'll try not to steal too much this year approach. How much do weddings cost?

Sit in staff meeting for two hours without having to say anything. Amazingly nobody asks me to say anything either. The other three seem to have a good time though. Try to listen hard to Pete's contributions to see if I could learn from them. He is younger and less experienced in ministry than me but he is ordained and I'm not. So the vicar listens to him. Mind you Pete does speak which must increase one's chances of being listened to, slightly.

Although we haven't done any formal announcing, the news of our engagement has more or less reached everyone now. People are pleased and encouraging. The old ladies in the church feel they have succeeded in their mission to marry me off to a nice young lady.

In the evening, Becca and I sit down and fix a date for our wedding. We opt for Easter next year. Looking through our diaries for the rest of this year we find we are both very busy but rarely at the same time. Even Christmas looks awkward because Becca will be going to stay with her family in a cottage they always use and I will have to be around to be on duty Christmas Eve, Christmas Day and New Year's Eve.

Realising that last Christmas we hadn't even met and next year we will get to call the shots we manage not to be too upset by this. We also book a few days together in early January, before school starts back.

October 31

Goodbye Ween. An investigation into the lighter side of the dark side with music, multimedia, testimony and symbolic acts. It takes me most of the day to get the church looking appropriate using some borrowed stage lighting, a smoke machine and 500 small candles.[4] It is packed with young people, many of whom have responded to an invitation issued through schools. Filling the church with slightly ambient drum 'n' bass makes the whole place feel more like a club with interesting architecture than a church. It is all we can do to get names and addresses and invite the young people to our more mainstream offerings at other times of the week.

Questions for October

1 Are there frustrations in your youth work that you can do very little without asking someone else for permission?

2 Do you agree with Trudge? Is it possible to be organised and be able to respond quickly?

3 Do you feel that only committed Christians should have jobs to do in the church?

4 How important is 'atmosphere' for youth events? What are the limits in creating the right atmosphere? Is 'the lighter side of the dark side' possible? Or dangerous?

Weekend away

November

November 1

It took a long time to clear up last night. Got to bed at 1.00 am. A trip to the pub for lunch with Pete followed by a walk around the golf course and a cup of tea is really refreshing. The pub has a single variety hop beer on called Pumpkin Ale. It is delicious. A windy beer though, I discover later.

November 4

Saturday. Jobs to do around the house but on the whole a happier man than I normally am. I have a busy couple of weeks coming up and I am not looking forward to them. In fact I am not looking forward to work very much at all these days, apart from face-to-face contact with young people, which I am loving.

November 5

In Brian, we play the truth game. Each member must make three statements, one of which is a lie and two true. Others have to write down which they think is the lie. A prize is won by the best detector of lies and the best liar. It goes well. Then we talk about Jesus the way and the truth.

In the ten minutes at the end of the meeting, before church has finished because someone is preaching for too long, I raise the matter of re-changing the name Brian. It is dismissed as a ridiculous idea. They love going to a group called Brian now. They want T-shirts made with 'I'm a Brian' on them.

We soul-searched for a long time at various committees before deciding that we would have a church bonfire party after the evening service. We do and it is fun. One of the first all-age events at which old and young mix reasonably well. The young are slightly better behaved than the old. As usual.

November 6

A busy day preparing for the training day tomorrow for full-time youth workers and their clergy. The Archbishop of Canterbury is to be the guest speaker. I am doing a workshop on 'Relationships between clergy and youth workers'. Wish I wasn't.

November 7

The day goes well. It is an enormous church set-up with many employees around. One of the rooms we are due to use is being decorated, but the two guys working there seem unperturbed by our request that it be put back in order, including refitting the lighting, within four hours. They get on with it as if it is a normal part of the way their employer deals with deadlines.

It is really good that the Archbishop gives his blessing to alternative worship and full-time youth ministry. He has a vision, he says, of '… a youth congregation in every town and city.'

My workshop goes the better for me being vulnerable and confessing that my relationship with my vicar could be better (for instance, it could exist). Lots of questions lead to a list of things the full-time youth workers would like their clergy to understand and vice versa. I think it is a profitable hour. I for one learn that many others are in the same boat as me.

Full-time youth ministry has arisen from the grass roots upwards not by some edict from on high. As a result nobody is setting the agenda for things such as pay and conditions, career structure, minimum training requirements or even selection procedure. I hope that the organisers of the conference will be able to pass my sheets of flip chart paper on to someone who can do something useful with them.[1]

November 8

A bishop from Northern Ireland, a friend of my vicar, is coming to visit our parish for a few days and to preach on Sunday. I am delegated to meet him from the airport. You don't see a bishop for years and then two come at once.

It is easy greeting a bishop at the airport. You don't have to stand around searching for him, he should be the old guy in purple. He is.

Take the bishop back to my place for a cup of tea before dropping him off at the vicarage. He says there is a bathroom in his house that is bigger than the whole of the first floor of mine. He's not bragging but remarking on how unfair it is. We are both single men in ministry. I end up defending his palatial life because he has to entertain more important people than I do. He tells me I am a good man. That's nice.

November 9

We are taking the young people away for the weekend tomorrow. It has been in my diary for ages and the venue has been booked for ever but preparation has consisted only of asking my co-leaders to run a teaching session each and booking a minibus. I need to check bedroom allocation, deliver the kids a kit list by hand and buy food.

November 10

Instead of a day off it is manic 'collect games stuff up' day. Then 20 kids, five leaders and two small children are packed into a minibus and two cars to spend a weekend awake. At midnight I am playing a torch-lit wide game. At 2 am, I turn the dormitory lights off for the third time.

November 11

The first noises of the morning happen at 6.45 am. It is the sound of teenage girls talking in the showers. This rouses me and some of the lighter sleeping lads so I resign myself to the end of sleep and get up to make bacon butties for everyone. Find that someone else is already doing it. Brilliant. I have the only food hygiene certificate on the team so we have crossed that fine line between acting as an institution and a family. As long as nobody dies we'll be OK.[2]

The day is spent in vigorous outdoor pursuits including my first go at mountain biking for about five years. The teaching goes well (we are doing Philippians). Its emphasis on harmonious Christian living is appropriate for a group crammed together into a small, former youth hostel with poor heating.

Some of the kids help cook and wash up without my needing to make rotas. Bedtime happens spontaneously at midnight.

November 12

The young people themselves devise a morning service to include the last chapter of Philippians. It is short, simple and inclusive. The small children (leaders' kids) entertain us by dancing in one of the songs. When we laugh they think it is with them not at them so they dance more so we laugh more. Thomas (aged 3) tells us jokes. He doesn't quite understand that every joke needs a punchline. He thinks all he has to do is ask a question and get someone to say, 'I don't know.' He hasn't got beyond saying, 'I don't know' himself. This makes his jokes much funnier.

'Why did the duck?'

'I don't know, Thomas, why did the duck?'

'I don't know.'

Crazy laughter all round. Lack of sleep makes funny things funnier and bad things er, badder.

We return in time for the evening service. The bishop tells us all to turn to our neighbour and tell them (it is a him in my case) how special they are. I hate it when asked to do this; especially in public. I manage it insincerely. The bishop manages to deal with lots of subjects that the passage (Ephesians 5) is not about and fails to deal with issues of headship and gender identity. He even has a drop kick at homosexuality on the way, despite the fact that it is not mentioned in the passage. Most of St Mary's regular preachers seem to have caught the bug of having a topic of the week and getting it out of the passage somehow. Some of the young people don't manage to be awake at the end of the sermon.

November 13

I have a review session with Sarah this morning in place of the regular staff meeting (Pete and vicar at clergy conference). Can't fault her. I bet she's even nice to animals. I have a date to speak at a school Christian Union at lunchtime. Sarah comes with me and tells two short stories which are both excellent – one about herself and one about Jesus.

On the way home, we have an interesting discussion about the usefulness of Christian Unions. We conclude that they are good as a fuelling point for evangelism and as a support group; they are worst when they are an excuse for the Christians in a school not to engage with the real world.

Becca says she is tired. When she is at work, she is in public view all the time, the nature of school, whereas I get some shade. Even though eating with a bishop is work it is also relaxing, as long as I remember not to scratch my ear with the fork.

Go to bed at 9.00 pm.

November 14

There is an email message from a student who was at the evening sermon on Sunday and, I discover, is gay. She is finding the assumptions at St Mary's, that we are all heterosexual and married, a little threatening. I need to think through the pastoral considerations before replying. Can't believe I said that. Must be getting old.

My own thinking on the subject of gay relationships has been backed into a corner and I really need to sit down and sort it out.

Go to bed at 9.30 pm.

November 15

I have a cold and, although my chest is clear, I have some trouble breathing properly. I suspect an infection. Mentioning this to the doctor's receptionist I am given an appointment for two hours time. Must try that one again, although it will look a bit suspicious when I say, 'Actually, doctor, it's my leg...' Anyway I duck out of a meeting to go to see Dr Jolly and he gives me antibiotics, without further ado or even carrying out an examination.

November 17

A strange day off. I decide to do some DIY (fixing the towel rail in the bathroom) and the shopping and the ironing (whilst watching the video of *Twelve Monkeys*, proof that Bruce Wills can act) and then in the evening, Becca and I head off to the cinema to see an adventure that's low on plot and high on escapism.

November 18

Wedding across town. We have started taking notes about how things are done. I also note I have started to say 'we'. Ian and Kate have known each other for about six years but are still only 21. They have looked forward to this day for ages. They look very young. It is a great day. I preach adequately but the family think I'm brilliant, '... the best sermon we ever heard'. I enjoy their old church building, the atmosphere and the worship led by excellent musicians. The only problem is a ceilidh thingy in the evening, but Becca and I stay firmly fixed in the bar and chat away the hours. I am delighted we are compatible in the barn-dance loathing area.

November 19

Pete preaches on the theme of God and the remnant. He is excellent. Pete that is. God is excellent too but in a different way. I may be believing in God again, a bit.

Discover that someone I know has had a very serious heart attack at the age of 49. It is very worrying and for the next few days, all chest pains, however minor, will be taken more seriously.

November 20

I have to write some Bible study notes on Ecclesiastes for the youth small Sunday groups next term. It has become one of my favourite books. There is a load of desk clearing to do too. I start on Ecclesiastes in the staff meeting until all goes quiet and everyone is staring at me. Apparently I was asked a direct question but I have no idea what it was. I apologise and it sort of snaps me back into place. I make another small piece of progress back into being part of the team, the church and the world.

November 21

Bible study group on John's Gospel ends by praying as we wash each other's feet. I have discovered that I want to carry on praying but I don't want to pray in company because I don't feel able to say 'Amen' to many prayers these days. Lots of prayers seem to me to be fundamentally selfish. Only the youth group's prayers seem 'real'.

November 22

The preparation, which I want to do, is going slowly, for reasons I can't fathom. 'Everything is nonsense...' (Ecclesiastes 1:2 – CEV).

November 23

Still exchanging email with student troubled about sexuality. It is a therapeutic exercise. Email offers a chance to try out thoughts with more weight than a conversation but less than a letter or article. It is enjoyable and quick. I wonder if it really matters to God if two people of the same gender live together in commitment, love and mutual sexual gratification. If you take your definition of sexual intercourse as something only possible between a man and a woman then they are doing something less than that. Not sinful? Not so sinful? Not sure I'm ready to go public on this yet.[3]

November 24

After nearly four weeks, I go football training and enjoy an excellent hour of five-a-side at the local park. We have another game soon. Pretty tired at the end though.

Becca has decided to leave her church officially at the pre-Christmas services and start worshipping at St Mary's from January.

November 25

Becca is away visiting family for the weekend so I give today over to contemplation. This year, I have been out of the parish far more than I ever expected when I started this job, but those things have kept me sane. If I stop spending so much time helping other churches and organisations, I might be able to find time to get going on an open youth club project to try and bridge the gap between Christian young people and the local kids who hang around outside church. Decide to take this to the Youth Committee as a discussion item. They will have to limit the amount of outside invitations I can accept if I am to get things going next year.[4]

I have one more week's holiday owing to me and this is going to be it. I'm going alone and I'm not even telling my diary where.[5]

Questions for November

1 Do you think full-time youth workers should belong to a trade union?

2 Has legislation spoiled this type of youth work completely?

3 How can the church welcome the homosexually orientated? Who is setting our agenda? Tradition? Culture? The Bible? Are they mutually exclusive? Are your views different from your churches? What does the average member of the congregation think about it?

4 Do you think it is better for youth ministers to limit the amount of time they spend on outside activities?

5 Is it possible for anyone involved in ministry to take holidays at home?

Christmas

December

December 3

The youth group are taking the morning all-age service. I have left this to the other leaders during my holiday. It is short, more a children's service than all-age and there is a lot of badly handled swapping around of microphones. Ben, Harry and Chris manage a dramatic, three-part reading very well though.

December 4

The Youth Committee debates lots of ideas about future direction, especially the open youth club idea. During the course of the conversation I notice that I am vacillating between opinions. Maybe I am simply good at seeing both sides of an argument. I don't sit on the fence, but I lean on it and think both directions look interesting.

James, who is at his first meeting, won't let me get away with this and constantly asks me for my opinion, '... as the expert here'. He is very forceful. He also says that if anything we want to do will cost money he thinks he can lay his hands on some sponsorship. I suspect this is his roundabout way of hiding his own generosity but it looks promising as well as humble. I am constantly frustrated that I have a reasonable youth budget but must get permission to spend it.[1]

I mention to James that the fund to support Sarah on her gap year is a bit low and he says he'll see what he can do.

December 5

The evening begins with young people, John 14 and a massive discussion about whether there is a way to know God through other religions, which doesn't involve knowing him as father. If Christianity is unique then are all other faiths bogus?

The end of the evening sees me again at Rob and Trudy's house, this time sorting through and re-editing our camp leaders' handbook. We always accompany these business meetings with a bottle of wine, one of the things that makes them bearable, but decisions taken later on in an evening occasionally need to be revisited.

December 6

Today I sit through nearly six hours of meetings. As a person who does meetings on 'override', that is to say I am suppressing my desire to go mad in groups of people, six hours is too long. Six hours leaves me yawning, contributing to discussions to entertain myself (after learning not to be quiet) and making up anagrams of the names of the participants.

We have extended staff time (1–4 pm), then I have a meeting with the Council about grants for youth work (5–6 pm) followed by a meeting with the wardens to discuss the way young people treat property (7–9 pm).

On the short drive home from Jack's (church warden) house, I break my car indicator by rearranging a pheasant. Spectacularly and bone-crunchingly.

Being bored and not tired I shave off my beard and moustache.

December 7

More bored so go to Frizz! and see if Ems can fit me in for a chat, oops I mean haircut. Before I have thought about it I am having shampoo rubbed into my scalp for the first time in months. Have to start again with that.

December 10

Nobody at church comments on my shave and shorter hair, although people seem to be looking at me in a 'what's different' sort of way.

In the evening, the youth group are catering for 50 people at a church function. I am in charge. Several people at church don't seem to be able to cope with the idea of a man being in charge of cooking (especially this one). Apart from a minor problem when we lose a vegetarian pizza, all goes well.

December 12

How many colds is it normal to have in a year? Becca has the cold of the year and is (gasp!) considering having a sicky tomorrow. I have flu-like symptoms.

Go to the local at lunchtime to mope and read the *Sun*. All youth workers should read the *Sun* once a month minimum. A good discussion question is, 'Does the *Sun* think sex is a good or bad thing?' It's not as easy a question as it sounds. I drink two halves of Drayman's Tipple, a single variety hop with the smell of whiskey about it. It gets to the cold fast.

I take the afternoon off sick.

December 13

I manage a whole heap of catch-up today which pleases me greatly. It includes getting stuck into a few of the Christmas sketches I have been planning for ages. Whilst distracted, I also produce a sketch about saying 'NO'. Seven ways to be negative, positively:

Decisive ambivalence I don't care and I'm certain about that.
Structured apathy This committee has decided to take no action.
Creative lethargy The problem will improve by being ignored (high risk but very effective if you can pull it off).
Negative encouragement May I encourage you not to do that again.
Instant procrastination I can tell you now that I'm not sure.
Enthusiastic reticence That sounds a very exciting idea; I'm sure there must be some good in it.
Hesitant synergy X is a great idea; how does it relate to Y?

December 16

Played footie. We won 3-1, all the goals coming in the first twenty minutes. It was a cold day and a frosty pitch (almost dangerous) and so I was covered in scratches and bruises by the end of the game.

Once married Becca and I will have 124 duplicate CDs or records and 35 duplicate novels. Decide to auction them for church funds as a thank offering.

December 17

Our church must have entered the 'How much can you pack into one service?' competition. Today's example: Holy Communion, baptism, launch of another new evangelistic initiative and farewell to a member of the congregation heading off to Africa for a year. It is well into one and a half hours and certainly half an hour beyond the heater timer. The thought of 'overseas' bugs me, not for the first time.

I promise to be at a meeting in the afternoon to think through our next piece of alternative worship, but this is before Harry tells me that I am the solution to his under-16s transport problem. 'I'll do you a deal Trudge. You give me and my mates a lift to our away game and we'll give you nothing.' Can't argue with business acumen like that.

A lift to the game, a decision not to watch it, the drive back to pick them up, watching the last of the four goals they concede go in and oh no I've forgotten the meeting.

I phone and apologise. Pete is accepting but sounds irritated too. So he's human.

December 18

Two traditionally Christmassy things happen today. Firstly we have a practice for the music group at Sunday morning's all-age carol service. I have agreed to hit my drums again. Secondly the staff team and partners head over to the vicarage for a pre-Christmas nosh up. It is great, but predictable, and Becca is still not well so we don't stay as late as we feared we had to. She has three Christmas things to go to this week at her school.

December 19

Staff prayer day. A good thing in a busy week. Don't now why we do it now but this church has had a pre-Christmas staff prayer day since BC. Then an evening drink with Dave and Trish who I have hardly seen for months. They are disappointed not to have met Becca yet. The beer is called Snowman's Revenge – an excellent name for a pre-Christmas drink.

December 20

At 5.50 am, I am wide awake due to a coughing fit. Wake up and drink coffee and read. Discover it is only 4.50 am. Go back to bed after half an hour. Fail to reset the alarm clock properly, take an hour to get back to sleep and then oversleep. It has been raining for a week non-stop. My shoes leak. I have a sore toe from last Saturday's football.

December 21

Christians stole the mid-winter solstice festival and so we do not need to put the Christ back into Christmas, we need to continue the process of putting Christ into Christmas for the first time. A little more positive, I reckon.

December 22

A couple of pints of Snowman's Revenge each (Becca drinks pints too) as a break from shopping and all is well with the world.[2] I am ending the year broke but happy. We're getting married next year.

December 24

Someone ought to send our church leaders on a theology course. Our service for the fourth Sunday in Advent is a mixture of Nativity and Epiphany. We have a huge mural of wise men (at least there are only two of them so someone accepts the possibility that one brought two gifts and the other one) on camels looking across at a star over Bethlehem. This is not what the Bible says.

At least the sermon, which is trivial pants, gives me a memorable expression, 'Kissing the trimmings', which I think describes Christmas very well. The music was good too.

I'm preaching at the midnight Holy Communion. The sheer joy and wonder of Christmas. I'm almost visibly shaken at how happy everybody is. Only joking. It contains the most sober, unresponsive congregation I have ever come across. They all seem to be there out of a sense of duty and I gauge the best way to keep them happy is to tell them a few things they want to hear, briefly, so that the whole show is over in an hour.

December 25

It's a happy day, Christmas Day. Although my ministry tradition is to take Christmas on the chin and really enjoy Boxing Day, this year Christmas is all right. Spend a pleasant afternoon and evening watching television alone, reading old newspapers and drinking an excellent single malt. Miss Becca but manage to speak to her on the phone.

December 26

Drive to my folks. My mum and dad are OKish, not listening and then saying I never tell them anything. Somehow the Boxing Day Christmas lunch is only half an hour later than Mum intended.

Ask Mum if I can put freezer labels on the pieces of furniture Becca and I want when they pop their clogs. Not a titter! My brother and his partner have avoided Christmas at home by going on a winter holiday.

December 27

Relaxing breakfast. I've got three excellent new books to read. I almost want to read them all at once. Drive home.

Old friend Ron, back in the country for a while, turns up for a drink in the evening, finishing off my scotch and not wanting his furniture back (see January).

I am unmotivated by the youth group preparation I need to do for a New Year's Eve party. I am still struggling with the whole big picture of Christianity but my job and house are attached to it very tightly.[3] I have no money.

December 28

Today I was cut up at a traffic island by a friend. He stopped ahead of me at the next set of lights, shaking his head from side to side as if I was a nutter. It was funny watching his expression change as he recognised me. He has blood pressure problems. I can see why.

December 31

Having started the year with a strange display at an all-age service I end it by preaching at another one. Again it is at St Mary's but this time, due to heating system failure, it is held in the hall which makes for an altogether more fun atmosphere. For an all-age service, we are a bit short of children.

The youth group party includes food and drink and music and chat and games and not dancing or strip poker. It will probably cause trouble but I end up playing cards with some of the lads for cash. They are paying a small amount of money for entertainment. If they weren't with me they'd be somewhere more expensive. So it's fun and not gambling. I seem to be getting my retaliatory argument in before the criticism has arrived. The Derby County motto – equalise before your opponents score.

I sub Harry for three hands and after that he pays me back and cleans everybody else out. A good summary of the whole year I think. I had hoped to try and explain the Church of England. To be honest I think I got bored with it. I may have spent a year explaining me.[4]

As we all wrote in junior school essays, 'And that is what I did last year. Goodbye.'

Remember, as my friend Simon told me, 'A poinsettia is for life, not just for Christmas.'[5]

Questions for December

1 Can your youth team spend the church's money without asking?

2 Do you think Trudge over-relies on alcohol to make the world OK?

3 Trudge has had a lot of doubts about his faith. At what point does doubt become unbelief?

4 If yor church had a vacancy for a youth worker, would you consider employing Trudge?

5 Revisit some of the earlier questions in the book. In the light of what you now know about Trudge, have you changed any of your opinions?